TO

_____

FROM

_____

LIVING WORDS OF JESUS

NEW LIVING
TRANSLATION

Living
Words
of *Jesus*

TYNDALE HOUSE PUBLISHERS, INC.
WHEATON, ILLINOIS

Visit Tyndale's exciting Web site at www.tyndale.com

Notes are adapted from the *Life Application Study Bible* copyright
© 1988, 1989, 1990, 1991, 1993, 1996 by Tyndale House Publishers, Inc. Wheaton, IL 60189. All rights reserved.

Scriptures compiled by Mark Norton

Living Words of Jesus

Copyright © 1997 Tyndale House Publishers, Inc.
All rights reserved.

Scripture quotations are taken from the *Holy Bible,* New Living
Translation, copyright © 1996. Used by permission of Tyndale
House Publishers, Inc., Wheaton, Illinois 60189. All rights
reserved.

ISBN: 0-8423-3249-9

Printed in the United States

03 02 01 00 99 98 97
8   7   6   5   4   3   2

CONTENTS

TO THE READER

Who is Jesus? Over the centuries he's been called everything from a wise teacher to a heretic to the Savior of the world.

In *Living Words of Jesus*, we have assembled the words of Jesus from the four books of the Bible that tell the story of his life: the Gospels of Matthew, Mark, Luke, and John. Organized by topic, this book allows you to investigate what Jesus said about himself and other topics. Short notes after each verse explain the culture, history, and background behind the saying.

Each verse in *Living Words of Jesus* is written in the New Living Translation. Based on the most recent scholarship and theory in translation, the New Living Translation is easy to read and understand while accurately communicating the meaning of the original text.

We hope that Jesus Christ's words will speak to your heart and you will continue your study of his life and work.

ONE SOLITARY LIFE

He was born in an obscure village, the child of a peasant woman. He grew up in another village. He worked in a carpenter shop until he was thirty and then for three years was an itinerant preacher. He never wrote a book. He never held an office. He never owned a home. He never traveled two hundred miles from the place where he was born. He never did one of the things that usually accompany greatness. He had no credentials but himself.

Although he walked the land over, curing the sick, giving sight to the blind, healing the lame, and raising people from the dead, the top established religious leaders turned against him. His friends ran away. He was turned over to enemies. He went through the mockery of a trial. He was spat upon, flogged, and ridiculed. He was nailed to a cross between two thieves. While he was dying, the executioners gambled for the only piece of property he had on earth, and that was his robe. When he was dead, he was laid in a borrowed grave through the pity of a friend.

Nineteen wide centuries have come and gone, and today he is the central Figure of the human race and the Leader of the column of progress.

All the armies that ever marched, and all the navies that were ever built, and all the parliaments that ever sat, and all the kings that ever reigned, put together, have not affected the life of man upon this earth as has that One Solitary Life.

—*Source Unknown*

The Person
of Jesus

THE IDENTITY OF JESUS

"I am the bread of life. No one who comes
to me will ever be hungry again. Those
who believe in me will never thirst. But you
haven't believed in me even though you
have seen me. However, those the Father
has given me will come to me, and I will
never reject them. For I have come down
from heaven to do the will of God who
sent me, not to do what I want. And this is
the will of God, that I should not lose even
one of all those he has given me, but that I
should raise them to eternal life at the last
day. For it is my Father's will that all who

see his Son and believe in him should have eternal life—that I should raise them at the last day." *John 6:35-40*

Jesus did not work independently of God the Father but in union with him. This should give us even more assurance of being welcomed into God's presence and being protected by him. Jesus' purpose was to do the will of God, not to satisfy Jesus' human desires. When we follow Jesus, we should have the same purpose.

"I am the light of the world. If you follow me, you won't be stumbling through the darkness, because you will have the light that leads to life." *John 8:12*

When Jesus said this, he was speaking in the part of the Temple where the offerings were put, where candles burned to symbolize the pillar of fire that led the people of Israel through the wilderness (Exodus 13:21-22). In this context, Jesus called himself the light of the world. The pillar of fire represented God's presence, protection, and guidance. Jesus brings God's presence, protection, and guidance. Is he the light of *your* world?

"I have come as a light to shine in this dark world, so that all who put their trust in me will no longer remain in the darkness."
John 12:46

As a soldier follows his captain, so we should follow Christ, our commander. As a slave follows his master, so we should follow Christ, the Lord. As we follow the advice of a trusted counselor, so we should follow Jesus' commands to us in Scripture. As we follow the laws of our nation, so we should follow the laws of the Kingdom of Heaven.

"I assure you, I am the gate for the sheep. . . . All others who came before me were thieves and robbers. But the true sheep did not listen to them. Yes, I am the gate. Those who come in through me will be saved. Wherever they go, they will find green pastures." *John 10:7-9*

In the sheepfold, the shepherd functioned as a gate, letting the sheep in and protecting them. Jesus is the gate to God's salvation for us. He offers access to safety and security. Some people resent that Jesus is the gate, the only access to God. But Jesus is God's Son—why should we seek any other way or want to customize a different approach to God?

"I am the good shepherd. The good shepherd lays down his life for the sheep. A hired hand will run when he sees a wolf coming. He will leave the sheep because they aren't his and he isn't their shepherd. And so the wolf attacks them and scatters the flock. The hired hand runs away because he is merely hired and has no real concern for the sheep.

"I am the good shepherd; I know my own sheep, and they know me, just as my Father knows me and I know the Father. And I lay down my life for the sheep." *John 10:11-15*

A hired hand tends the sheep for money, while the shepherd does it out of love. The

shepherd owns the sheep and is committed
to them. Jesus is not merely doing a job; he
is committed to loving us and even laying
down his life for us. False teachers and
prophets do not have this commitment.

"I am the resurrection and the life. Those
who believe in me, even though they die
like everyone else, will live again. They are
given eternal life for believing in me and
will never perish." *John 11:25-26*

Jesus has power over life and death as well
as power to forgive sins. This is because
he is the creator of life. He who *is* life can
surely restore life. Whoever believes in
Christ has a spiritual life that death cannot
conquer or diminish in any way. When we
realize his power and how wonderful his
offer to us really is, how can we not commit our life to him?

"I am the way, the truth, and the life. No
one can come to the Father except through
me. If you had known who I am, then you

would have known who my Father is. From now on you know him and have seen him!"
John 14:6-7

> Jesus says he is the only way to God the Father. Some people may argue that this way is too narrow. In reality, it is wide enough for the whole world, if the world chooses to accept it. Instead of worrying about how limited it sounds to have only one way, we should be saying, "Thank you, God, for providing a sure way to get to you!"

"If you trust me, you are really trusting God who sent me. For when you see me, you are seeing the one who sent me. I have come as a light to shine in this dark world, so that all who put their trust in me will no longer remain in the darkness." *John 12:44-46*

> We often wonder what God is like. How can we know the Creator when he doesn't make himself visible? Jesus said plainly that those who see him see God, because he *is* God. If you want to know what God is like, study the person and words of Jesus Christ.

"I am the true vine, and my Father is the gardener. He cuts off every branch that doesn't produce fruit, and he prunes the branches that do bear fruit so they will produce even more. You have already been pruned for greater fruitfulness by the message I have given you. Remain in me, and I will remain in you. For a branch cannot produce fruit if it is severed from the vine, and you cannot be fruitful apart from me. . . .

"Yes, I am the vine; you are the branches. Those who remain in me, and I in them, will produce much fruit. For apart from me you can do nothing." *John 15:1-5*

Christ is the vine, and God is the gardener who cares for the branches to make them fruitful. The branches are all those who claim to be followers of Christ.

Jesus makes a distinction between two kinds of pruning: (1) cutting off and (2) cutting back branches. Fruitful branches are cut back to promote growth. In other words, God must sometimes discipline us to strengthen our character and faith. But branches that don't bear fruit are cut off at the trunk not only because they are worthless but also because they often infect the rest of the tree. People who don't bear fruit for God or who try to block the efforts of God's followers will be cut off from this life-giving power.

"Do you believe in the Son of Man? . . . You have seen him, and he is speaking to you!" *John 9:35, 37*

The "Son of Man" is Jesus himself. This title "Son of Man" occurs many times in the New Testament in reference to Jesus as the Messiah.

"I am not an earthly king. If I were, my followers would have fought when I was arrested by the Jewish leaders. But my Kingdom is not of this world." *John 18:36*

In this verse, Jesus is responding to Pilate. There seems to have been no question in Pilate's mind that Jesus spoke the truth and

was innocent of any crime. It also seems
apparent that, while recognizing the truth,
Pilate chose to reject it. It is a great tragedy
when we recognize the truth but fail to
heed it.

JESUS AND THE FATHER

"I assure you, the Son can do nothing by himself. He does only what he sees the Father doing. Whatever the Father does, the Son also does. For the Father loves the Son and tells him everything he is doing, and the Son will do far greater things than healing this man. You will be astonished at what he does. He will even raise from the dead anyone he wants to, just as the Father does." *John 5:19-21*

Because of his unity with God, Jesus lived as God wanted him to live. Because of our identification with Jesus, we must honor him and live as he wants us to live. The questions "What would Jesus do?" and "What would Jesus have me do?" may help us make the right choices.

"Since you don't know who I am, you don't know who my Father is. If you knew me, then you would know my Father, too." *John 8:19*

Jesus and the Father are one.

"The Father and I are one." *John 10:30*

This is the clearest statement of Jesus' divinity he ever made. Jesus and his Father are not the same person, but they are one in essence and nature. Thus, Jesus is not merely a good teacher—he is God. His claim to be God was unmistakable. The religious leaders wanted to kill him because their laws said that anyone claiming to be God should die. Nothing could persuade them that Jesus' claim was true.

"Truly, anyone who welcomes my messenger is welcoming me, and anyone who

welcomes me is welcoming the Father who sent me." *John 13:20*

> When people welcome our proclamations of the Good News, they are also welcoming Jesus Christ and, through him, the Father.

"Philip, don't you even yet know who I am, even after all the time I have been with you? Anyone who has seen me has seen the Father! So why are you asking to see him? Don't you believe that I am in the Father and the Father is in me? The words I say are not my own, but my Father who lives in me does his work through me. Just believe that I am in the Father and the Father is in me. Or at least believe because of what you have seen me do." *John 14:9-11*

> Jesus is the visible, tangible image of the invisible God. He is the complete revelation of what God is like. Jesus explained to Philip, who wanted to see the Father, that to know Jesus is to know God. The search for God, for truth and reality, ends in Christ.

THE AUTHORITY OF JESUS

"Is it easier to say, 'Your sins are forgiven' or 'Get up and walk'? I will prove that I, the Son of Man, have the authority on earth to forgive sins." Then Jesus turned to the paralyzed man and said, "Stand up, take your mat, and go on home, because you are healed!"
Matthew 9:5-6

It's easy to tell someone his sins are forgiven; it's a lot more difficult to reverse a case of paralysis! Jesus backed up his words by healing the man's legs. Jesus' action showed that his words were true; he had the power to forgive as well as to heal. Our words lack meaning if our actions do not back them up. We can say we love God or others, but if we are not taking practical steps to demonstrate that love, our words are empty and meaningless.

"And haven't you ever read in the law of Moses that the priests on duty in the Temple may work on the Sabbath? . . .

"For I, the Son of Man, am master even of the Sabbath." *Matthew 12:5, 8*

When Jesus said he was master of the Sabbath, he claimed to be greater than the law and above the law. To the Pharisees, this was heresy. They did not realize that Jesus, the divine Son of God, had created the Sabbath. The creator is always greater than his creation; thus, Jesus had the authority to overrule the Pharisees' traditions and regulations.

"Don't you realize that I could ask my Father for thousands of angels to protect us, and he would send them instantly? But if I did, how would the Scriptures be fulfilled

that describe what must happen now?"
Matthew 26:53-54

> Jesus said this in response to Peter, who
> had cut off the servant's ear in Gethsem-
> ane. Peter was trying to prevent the arrest
> of Jesus, which he saw as defeat. He didn't
> realize that Jesus had to die in order to
> gain victory. But Jesus demonstrated per-
> fect commitment to his Father's will. His
> Kingdom would not be advanced with
> swords but with faith and obedience.

"But I do nothing without consulting the
Father. I judge as I am told. And my judgment is absolutely just, because it is according to the will of God who sent me; it is not
merely my own.

"If I were to testify on my own behalf, my
testimony would not be valid. But someone
else is also testifying about me, and I can
assure you that everything he says about me
is true. In fact, you sent messengers to listen
to John the Baptist, and he preached the
truth. But the best testimony about me is

not from a man, though I have reminded you about John's testimony so you might be saved. John shone brightly for a while, and you benefited and rejoiced. But I have a greater witness than John—my teachings and my miracles. They have been assigned to me by the Father, and they testify that the Father has sent me. And the Father himself has also testified about me. You have never heard his voice or seen him face to face, and you do not have his message in your hearts, because you do not believe me—the one he sent to you." *John 5:30-38*

In his testimony Jesus claimed to be equal with God, to give eternal life, to be the source of life, and to judge sin. These statements make it clear that Jesus was claiming to be divine—an almost unbelievable claim, but one that was supported by another witness, John the Baptist.

THE MISSION OF JESUS

"Healthy people don't need a doctor—
sick people do. . . . Now go and learn the
meaning of this Scripture: 'I want you to
be merciful; I don't want your sacrifices.'
For I have come to call sinners, not those
who think they are already good enough."
Matthew 9:12-13

> Those who are sure that they are good
> enough can't be saved because the first step
> in following Jesus is acknowledging our sins
> and admitting that we don't have all the
> answers.

"The Spirit of the Lord is upon me,
   for he has appointed me to preach Good
      News to the poor.
He has sent me to proclaim
   that captives will be released,
   that the blind will see,
   that the downtrodden will be freed from
      their oppressors,
   and that the time of the Lord's favor has
      come . . .
"This Scripture has come true today
before your very eyes!" *Luke 4:18-19, 21*

Jesus was quoting from Isaiah 61:1-2. Isaiah pictures the deliverance of Israel from exile in Babylon as a Year of Jubilee, a time when all debts are cancelled, all slaves are freed, and all property is returned to its original owners (Leviticus 25). But the release from Babylonian exile had not brought the fulfillment the people had expected; they were still a conquered and oppressed people. So Isaiah must have been referring to a future messianic age. Jesus boldly announced, "This Scripture has come true today

before your very eyes!" Jesus was proclaim-
ing himself as the one who would bring
this Good News to pass but in a way that
the people would not yet be able to grasp.

"I have come to bring fire to the earth,
and I wish that my task were already com-
pleted! There is a terrible baptism ahead
of me, and I am under a heavy burden
until it is accomplished. Do you think I
have come to bring peace to the earth?
No, I have come to bring strife and division! From now on families will be split
apart, three in favor of me, and two
against—or the other way around. There
will be a division between father and son,
mother and daughter, mother-in-law and
daughter-in-law." *Luke 12:49-53*

By these strange and unsettling words, Jesus
revealed that his coming often results in conflict. Because he demands a response, families
may be split apart when some choose to
follow him and others refuse to do so. There
is no middle ground with Jesus. He demands

loyalty and commitment, sometimes to the point of severing other relationships. Are you willing to risk your family's disapproval in order to gain eternal life?

"My nourishment comes from doing the will of God, who sent me, and from finishing his work." *John 4:34*

The "food" about which Jesus was speaking was his spiritual nourishment. It includes more than Bible study, prayer, and attending church. Spiritual nourishment also comes from doing God's will and helping to bring his work of salvation to completion. We are nourished not only by what we take in but also by what we give out for God.

"Now my soul is deeply troubled. Should I pray, 'Father, save me from what lies ahead'? But that is the very reason why I came! Father, bring glory to your name." *John 12:27-28*

Jesus knew that his crucifixion lay ahead, and because he was human, he dreaded it. He knew he would have to take the sins of the world on himself, and he knew this would separate him from his Father. He wanted to be delivered from this horrible death, but he knew that God had sent him into the world to die in our place for our sins. Jesus said no to his human desires in order to obey his Father and glorify him. Although we will never have to face such a difficult and awesome task, we are still called to obedience. Whatever the Father asks, we should do his will and bring glory to his name.

JESUS AND THE CHILDREN

"Anyone who wants to be the first must take last place and be the servant of everyone else."

Then he put a little child among them. Taking the child in his arms, he said to them, "Anyone who welcomes a little child like this on my behalf welcomes me, and anyone who welcomes me welcomes my Father who sent me." *Mark 9:35-37*

> Jesus taught the disciples to welcome children. This was a new approach in a society where children were usually treated as second-class citizens. It is important not only

to treat children well but also to teach them about Jesus. Children's ministries should never be regarded as less important than those for adults.

"O Father, Lord of heaven and earth, thank you for hiding the truth from those who think themselves so wise and clever, and for revealing it to the childlike. Yes, Father, it pleased you to do it this way!" *Matthew 11:25-26*

Jesus mentioned two kinds of people in his prayer: the "wise and clever"—arrogant in their own knowledge—and the "childlike"—humbly open to receive the truth of God's Word. Are you wise in your own eyes, or do you seek the truth in childlike faith, realizing that only God holds all the answers?

"I assure you, unless you turn from your sins and become as little children, you will never get into the Kingdom of Heaven. Therefore, anyone who becomes as humble as this little child is the greatest in the Kingdom of Heaven. *Matthew 18:3-5*

The disciples had become so preoccupied
with the organization of Jesus' earthly kingdom that they had lost sight of its divine purpose. Instead of seeking a place of service,
they sought positions of advantage. It is easy
to lose our eternal perspective and compete
for promotions or status in the church. It is difficult to identify with "children"—weak and
dependent people with no status or influence.

**"Anyone who welcomes a little child like
this on my behalf is welcoming me. But if
anyone causes one of these little ones who
trusts in me to lose faith, it would be better
for that person to be thrown into the sea
with a large millstone tied around the neck."**
Matthew 18:5-6

Children are trusting by nature. Because
they trust adults, they are easily led to faith
in Christ. God holds parents and other
adults accountable for how they influence
these little ones. Jesus warned that anyone
who turns little children away from faith in
him will receive severe punishment.

"Let the children come to me. Don't stop them! For the Kingdom of Heaven belongs to such as these." *Matthew 19:14*

Jesus wanted little children to come to him because he loves them and because they have a guileless trust in God. He didn't mean that heaven is only for children but that all people need childlike faith in God. The receptiveness of little children was a great contrast to the stubbornness of the religious leaders, who let their education and sophistication stand in the way of the simple faith needed to believe in Jesus.

THE BODY AND BLOOD
OF JESUS

"Take it and eat it, for this is my body. . . .
Each of you drink from it, for this is my
blood, which seals the covenant between
God and his people. It is poured out to forgive the sins of many. Mark my words—I
will not drink wine again until the day I
drink it new with you in my Father's Kingdom." *Matthew 26:26-29*

> Each name we use for this sacrament
> brings out a different dimension to it. It is
> the *Lord's Supper* because it commemorates

the Passover meal Jesus ate with his disciples;
it is the *Eucharist* (thanksgiving) because in
it we thank God for Christ's work for us; it
is *Communion* because through it we com-
mune with God and with other believers.
As we eat the bread and drink the wine,
we should be quietly reflective as we recall
Jesus' death and his promise to come again,
grateful for God's wonderful gift to us, and
joyful as we meet with Christ and the body
of believers.

"I assure you, Moses didn't give them bread
from heaven. My Father did. And now he
offers you the true bread from heaven."
John 6:32

People eat bread to satisfy physical hunger
and to sustain physical life. We can satisfy
spiritual hunger and sustain spiritual life only
by a right relationship with Jesus Christ—
that is why he called himself the bread of
life. But bread must be eaten to sustain life,
and Christ must be invited into our daily
walk to sustain spiritual life.

"I assure you, unless you eat the flesh of the Son of Man and drink his blood, you cannot have eternal life within you. But those who eat my flesh and drink my blood have eternal life, and I will raise them at the last day. For my flesh is the true food, and my blood is the true drink. All who eat my flesh and drink my blood remain in me, and I in them. I live by the power of the living Father who sent me; in the same way, those who partake of me will live because of me. I am the true bread from heaven. Anyone who eats this bread will live forever and not die as your ancestors did, even though they ate the manna." *John 6:53-58*

This was a shocking message—to eat flesh and drink blood sounded cannibalistic. The idea of drinking any blood, let alone human blood, was repugnant to the religious leaders because the law forbade it. Jesus was not talking about literal blood, of course. He was saying that his life had to become their own, but they could not accept this concept. The apostle Paul later used the body and blood imagery in talking about Communion.

Following

Jesus

THE CALL TO
FOLLOW JESUS

"Come, be my disciples, and I will show you how to fish for people!" *Mark 1:17*

> We often assume that Jesus' disciples were great men of faith from the first time they met Jesus. But they had to grow in their faith just as all believers do. Although it took time for Jesus' call and his message to get through, the disciples *followed.* We may question and falter just as they did, but we must never stop following Jesus.

"My light will shine out for you just a little while longer. Walk in it while you can, so you will not stumble when the darkness falls. If you walk in the darkness, you cannot see where you are going. Believe in the light while there is still time; then you will become children of the light." *John 12:35-36*

> Jesus said he would be with his followers in person for only a short time, and they should take advantage of his presence while they had it. Like a light shining in a dark place, he would point out the way they should walk. If they walked in his light, they would become "children of the light," revealing the truth and pointing people to God. As Christians, we are to be Christ's light bearers, letting his light shine through us. How brightly is your light shining? Can others see Christ in you?

"You are truly my disciples if you keep obeying my teachings. And you will know the truth, and the truth will set you free." *John 8:31-32*

Jesus himself is the truth that sets us free. He is the source of truth, the perfect standard of what is right. He frees us from the consequences of sin, from self-deception, and from Satan's deception. He shows us clearly the way to eternal life with God. Thus, Jesus does not give us freedom to do what we want but freedom to follow God. As we seek to serve God, Jesus' perfect truth frees us to be all that God meant us to be.

THE COST OF
FOLLOWING JESUS

"Foxes have dens to live in, and birds have nests, but I, the Son of Man, have no home of my own, not even a place to lay my head." *Matthew 8:20*

Following Jesus is not always easy or comfortable. Often it means great cost and sacrifice, with no earthly rewards or security. Jesus didn't have a place to call home. You may find that following Christ costs you popularity, friendships, leisure time, or treasured habits. But while the cost of following Christ is high, the value of being Christ's disciple is even higher. Discipleship is an investment that lasts for eternity and yields incredible rewards.

"Follow me now! Let those who are spiritually dead care for their own dead."
Matthew 8:22

Jesus was always direct with those who wanted to follow him. He made sure they counted the cost and set aside any conditions they might have for following him. As God's Son, Jesus did not hesitate to demand complete loyalty. Even family loyalty was not to take priority over the demands of obedience to him. His direct challenge forces us to ask ourselves about our own priorities in following him. The decision to follow Jesus should not be put off, even though other loyalties compete for our attention. Nothing should be placed above total commitment to living for him.

"If you refuse to take up your cross and follow me, you are not worthy of being mine."
Matthew 10:38

To take up our cross and follow Jesus means to be willing to publicly identify with him, to experience certain opposition, and to be willing to face even suffering and death for his sake.

"If you cling to your life, you will lose it; but if you give it up for me, you will find it."
Matthew 10:39

This verse is a positive and a negative statement of the same truth: Clinging to this life may cause us to forfeit the best from Christ in this world *and* in the next. The more we love this life's rewards (leisure, power, popularity, financial security), the more we will discover how empty they really are. The best way to enjoy life, therefore, is to loosen our greedy grasp on earthly rewards so we can be free to follow Christ. In doing so, we will inherit eternal life and begin at once to experience the benefits of following Christ.

"If any of you wants to be my follower, you must put aside your selfish ambition,

shoulder your cross daily, and follow me. If you try to keep your life for yourself, you will lose it. But if you give up your life for me, you will find true life. And how do you benefit if you gain the whole world but lose or forfeit your own soul in the process?" *Luke 9:23-25*

Christians follow their Lord by imitating his life and obeying his commands. In ancient times, to shoulder one's cross meant to carry one's own cross to the place of crucifixion. Many Galileans had been killed that way by the Romans. Applied to the disciples, it meant to identify completely with Christ's message, even if it meant death. Applied to us, it means that we must deny our selfish desires to use our time and money our own way and to choose our own direction in life without regard to Christ. Following Christ in this life may be costly, but in the long run it is well worth the pain and effort.

"If you want to be my follower you must love me more than your own father and mother, wife and children, brothers and sisters—yes, more than your own life. Otherwise, you cannot be my disciple. And you cannot be my disciple if you do not carry your own cross and follow me." *Luke 14:26-27*

Jesus' audience was well aware of what it meant to carry one's own cross. When the Romans led a criminal to his execution site, he was forced to carry the cross on which he would die. This showed his submission to Rome and warned observers that they had better submit too. Jesus taught this to get the crowds to think through their enthusiasm for him. He encouraged those who were superficial to either go deeper or turn back. Following Christ means total submission to him—perhaps even to the point of death.

"When a servant comes in from plowing or taking care of sheep, he doesn't just sit down and eat. He must first prepare his master's meal and serve him his supper before eating his own. And the servant is

not even thanked, because he is merely doing what he is supposed to do. In the same way, when you obey me you should say, 'We are not worthy of praise. We are servants who have simply done our duty.'"
Luke 17:7-10

> If we have obeyed God, we have only done our duty, and we should regard it as a privilege. Do you sometimes feel that you deserve extra credit for serving God? Remember, obedience is not something extra we do; it is our duty. Jesus is not suggesting that our service is meaningless or useless, nor is he advocating doing away with rewards. He is attacking unwarranted self-esteem and spiritual pride.

THE REWARDS OF
FOLLOWING JESUS

"And everyone who has given up houses
or brothers or sisters or father or mother
or children or property, for my sake, will
receive a hundred times as much in return
and will have eternal life. But many who
seem to be important now will be the least
important then, and those who are considered least here will be the greatest then."
Matthew 19:29-30

Jesus turned the world's values upside
down. In the life to come, the last will be
first. Don't ignore eternal rewards for

temporary benefits. Be willing to make sacrifices now for greater rewards later. Be willing to accept human disapproval while knowing that you have God's approval.

"And I assure you of this: If anyone acknowledges me publicly here on earth, I, the Son of Man, will openly acknowledge that person in the presence of God's angels."
Luke 12:8

We deny Jesus when we (1) hope no one will find out we are Christians, (2) decide *not* to speak up for what is right, (3) are silent about our relationship with God, (4) blend into society, and (5) accept our culture's non-Christian values. By contrast, we acknowledge him when we (1) live a moral, upright, Christ-honoring life, (2) look for opportunities to share our faith with others, (3) help others in need, (4) take a stand for justice, (5) love others, (6) acknowledge our loyalty to Christ, and (7) use our life and resources to carry out his desires rather than our own.

"My sheep recognize my voice; I know them, and they follow me.

"I give them eternal life, and they will never perish. No one will snatch them away from me, for my Father has given them to me, and he is more powerful than anyone else. So no one can take them from me."
John 10:27-29

> Just as a shepherd protects his sheep, Jesus protects his people from eternal harm. While believers can expect to suffer on earth, Satan cannot harm their souls or take away their eternal life with God. There are many reasons to be afraid here on earth because this is the Devil's domain. But if you choose to follow Jesus, he will give you everlasting safety.

THE AUTHORITY OF JESUS'
FOLLOWERS

"I tell you this: Whatever you prohibit on earth is prohibited in heaven, and whatever you allow on earth is allowed in heaven.

"I also tell you this: If two of you agree down here on earth concerning anything you ask, my Father in heaven will do it for you. For where two or three gather together because they are mine, I am there among them." *Matthew 18:18-20*

This *prohibiting* and *allowing* refers to the decisions of the church in conflicts. Among believers, there is no court of appeals beyond the church. Ideally, the church's decisions should be God-guided and based on discernment of his Word. Believers have the responsibility, therefore, to bring their problems to the church, and the church has the responsibility to use God's guidance in seeking to resolve conflicts. Handling problems God's way will have an impact now and for eternity.

"Go into all the world and preach the Good News to everyone, everywhere. Anyone who believes and is baptized will be saved. But anyone who refuses to believe will be condemned." *Mark 16:15-16*

Jesus told his disciples to go into all the world and tell everyone that he had paid the penalty for sin and that those who believe in him can be forgiven and live eternally with God. Do you ever feel as though you don't have the skill or determination to be a witness for Christ? You must personally realize that Jesus rose from the dead and lives for you today. As you grow in your relationship with Christ, he will give you both the opportunities and the inner strength to tell his message.

"I saw Satan falling from heaven as a flash of lightning! And I have given you authority over all the power of the enemy, and you can walk among snakes and scorpions and crush them. Nothing will injure you. But don't rejoice just because evil spirits obey you; rejoice because your names are registered as citizens of heaven." *Luke 10:18-20*

The disciples had seen tremendous results as they ministered in Jesus' name and with his authority. They were elated by the victories they had witnessed, and Jesus shared their enthusiasm. He helped them get their priorities right, however, by reminding them of their most important victory—that their names were registered in heaven. This honor was more important than any of their accomplishments. As we see God's wonders at work in and through us, we should not lose sight of the greatest wonder of all—our heavenly citizenship.

"The truth is, anyone who believes in me will do the same works I have done, and even greater works, because I am going to be with the Father. You can ask for anything in my name, and I will do it, because the work of the Son brings glory to the Father." *John 14:12-13*

> Jesus did not mean literally that his disciples would do greater works—after all, raising the dead is about as amazing as you can get. Rather, the disciples, working in the power of the Holy Spirit, would carry the Good News of God's Kingdom out of Palestine and into the whole world.

"Yes, ask anything in my name, and I will do it!" *John 14:14*

> When Jesus says we can ask for anything, we must remember that our asking must be in his name—that is, according to God's character and will. God will not grant requests

contrary to his nature or his will, and we cannot use his name as a magic formula to fulfill our selfish desires. If we are sincerely following God and seeking to do his will, then our requests will be in line with what he wants, and he will grant them.

THE MISSION OF JESUS'
FOLLOWERS

"You are the salt of the earth. But what
good is salt if it has lost its flavor? Can you
make it useful again? It will be thrown out
and trampled underfoot as worthless."
Matthew 5:13

> If a seasoning has no flavor, it has no value.
> If Christians make no effort to affect the
> world around them, they are of little value
> to God. If we are too much like the world,
> we are worthless. Christians should not
> blend in with everyone else. Instead, we

should affect others positively, just as seasoning brings out the best flavor in food.

"You are the light of the world—like a city on a mountain, glowing in the night for all to see. Don't hide your light under a basket! Instead, put it on a stand and let it shine for all. In the same way, let your good deeds shine out for all to see, so that everyone will praise your heavenly Father."
Matthew 5:14-16

If we live for Christ, we will glow like lights, showing others what Christ is like. Be a beacon of truth—don't shut your light off from the rest of the world.

"The harvest is so great, but the workers are so few. So pray to the Lord who is in charge of the harvest; ask him to send out more workers for his fields." *Matthew 9:37-38*

Jesus looked at the crowds following him and referred to them as a field ripe for harvest. Many people are ready to give their lives to Christ if someone would show them how. Jesus commands us to pray that people will respond to this need for workers. Often when we pray for something, God answers our prayers by using *us*. Be prepared for God to use you to show another person the way to him.

"My nourishment comes from doing the will of God, who sent me, and from finishing his work. Do you think the work of harvesting will not begin until the summer ends four months from now? Look around you! Vast fields are ripening all around us and are ready now for the harvest. The harvesters are paid good wages, and the fruit they harvest is people brought to eternal life. What joy awaits both the planter and the harvester alike! You know the saying, 'One person plants and someone else harvests.' And it's true. I sent you to harvest where you didn't plant; others had already done the work, and you will gather the harvest." *John 4:34-38*

Sometimes Christians excuse themselves from witnessing by saying that their family

or friends aren't ready to believe. Jesus,
however, makes it clear that around us a
continual harvest waits to be reaped. Don't
let Jesus find you making excuses. Look
around. You will find people ready to hear
God's Word.

"Go and announce to them that the Kingdom of Heaven is near. Heal the sick, raise
the dead, cure those with leprosy, and cast
out demons. Give as freely as you have
received!" *Matthew 10:7-8*

Jesus gave the disciples a principle to guide
their actions as they ministered to others:
"Give as freely as you have received." Because
God has showered us with his blessings, we
should give generously to others of our time,
love, and possessions.

"Look, I am sending you out as sheep
among wolves. Be as wary as snakes and
harmless as doves. But beware! For you will
be handed over to the courts and beaten in
the synagogues. And you must stand trial

before governors and kings because you are my followers. This will be your opportunity to tell them about me—yes, to witness to the world." *Matthew 10:16-18*

> The opposition of the Pharisees would be like ravaging wolves. The disciples' only hope would be to look to their Shepherd for protection. We may face similar hostility. Like the disciples, we are not to be sheeplike in our attitude but sensible and prudent. We are not to be gullible pawns, but neither are we to be deceitful connivers. We must find a balance between wisdom and vulnerability to accomplish God's work.

"Therefore, go and make disciples of all the nations, baptizing them in the name of the Father and the Son and the Holy Spirit. Teach these new disciples to obey all the commands I have given you. And be sure of this: I am with you always, even to the end of the age." *Matthew 28:19-20*

> Jesus' words affirm the reality of the Trinity. Some people accuse theologians of making

up the concept of the Trinity and reading it into Scripture. As we see here, the concept comes directly from Jesus himself. He did not say baptize them in the *names* but in the *name* of the Father, Son, and Holy Spirit. The word *Trinity* does not occur in Scripture, but it well describes the three-in-one nature of the Father, Son, and Holy Spirit.

"When the Holy Spirit has come upon you, you will receive power and will tell people about me everywhere—in Jerusalem, throughout Judea, in Samaria, and to the ends of the earth." *Acts 1:8*

Power from the Holy Spirit is not limited to strength beyond the ordinary. That power also involves courage, boldness, confidence, insight, ability, and authority. The disciples would need all these gifts to fulfill their mission. If you believe in Jesus Christ as your Savior, you can experience the power of the Holy Spirit in your life.

"The Good News about the Kingdom will be preached throughout the whole world, so that all nations will hear it; and then, finally, the end will come." *Matthew 24:14*

Jesus said that before he returns, the Good News about the Kingdom (the message of salvation) would be preached throughout the world. This was the disciples' mission— and it is ours today. Jesus talked about the end times and final judgment to show his followers the urgency of spreading the Good News of salvation to everyone.

SERVICE AND LEADERSHIP

"You know that in this world kings are tyrants, and officials lord it over the people beneath them. But among you it should be quite different. Whoever wants to be a leader among you must be your servant, and whoever wants to be first must become your slave. For even I, the Son of Man, came here not to be served but to serve others, and to give my life as a ransom for many." *Matthew 20:25-28*

Jesus described leadership from a new perspective. Instead of using people, we are to serve them. Jesus' mission was to

serve others and to give his life away. A
real leader has a servant's heart. Servant
leaders appreciate others' worth and realize that they're not above any job. If you
see something that needs to be done,
don't wait to be asked. Take the initiative
and do it like a faithful servant.

"The greatest among you must be a servant.
But those who exalt themselves will be
humbled, and those who humble themselves will be exalted." *Matthew 23:11-12*

Jesus challenged society's norms. To him,
greatness comes from serving—giving of
yourself to help God and others. Service
keeps us aware of others' needs, and it stops
us from focusing only on ourselves. Jesus
came as a servant. What kind of greatness
do you seek?

After they arrived at Capernaum, Jesus
and his disciples settled in the house
where they would be staying. Jesus asked
them, "What were you discussing out on

the road?" But they didn't answer, because they had been arguing about which of them was the greatest. He sat down and called the twelve disciples over to him. Then he said, "Anyone who wants to be the first must take last place and be the servant of everyone else." *Mark 9:33-35*

> In these verses, Jesus described leadership from a new perspective. Instead of using people, we are to serve them. Jesus' mission was to serve others and to give his life away. A real leader has a servant's heart.

After washing their feet, he put on his robe again and sat down and asked, "Do you understand what I was doing? You call me 'Teacher' and 'Lord,' and you are right, because it is true. And since I, the Lord and Teacher, have washed your feet, you ought to wash each other's feet. I have given you an example to follow. Do as I have done to you." *John 13:12-15*

> Jesus did not wash his disciples' feet just to get them to be nice to each other. His far

greater goal was to extend his mission on earth after he was gone. These men were to move into the world serving God, serving each other, and serving all people to whom they took the message of salvation.

Promises of

Jesus

COMFORT, PEACE, AND REST

"Come to me, all of you who are weary and carry heavy burdens, and I will give you rest. Take my yoke upon you. Let me teach you, because I am humble and gentle, and you will find rest for your souls. For my yoke fits perfectly, and the burden I give you is light." *Matthew 11:28-30*

A person may be carrying heavy burdens of (1) sin, (2) excessive demands of religious leadership, (3) oppression and persecution, or (4) weariness in the search for God. Jesus frees people from all these burdens. The rest that Jesus promises is love, healing, and peace with God, not the end of all labor. A relationship with God changes meaningless, wearisome toil into spiritual productivity and purpose.

"So I tell you, don't worry about everyday life—whether you have enough food to eat or clothes to wear. For life consists of far more than food and clothing. Look at the ravens. They don't need to plant or harvest or put food in barns because God feeds them. And you are far more valuable to him than any birds! Can all your worries add a single moment to your life? Of course not! And if worry can't do little things like that, what's the use of worrying over bigger things?

"Look at the lilies and how they grow. They don't work or make their clothing, yet Solomon in all his glory was not dressed as beautifully as they are. And if God cares so wonderfully for flowers that are here today and gone tomorrow, won't he more surely care for you? You have so little faith!"
Luke 12:22-28

Jesus commands us not to worry. But how can we avoid it? Only faith can free us from the anxiety caused by greed and covetousness. It is good to work and plan responsibly; it is bad to dwell on all the ways our planning could go wrong. Worry is pointless because it can't fill any of our needs; worry is foolish because the Creator of the universe loves us and knows what we need. He promises to meet all our real needs but not necessarily all our desires.

"I am leaving you with a gift—peace of mind and heart. And the peace I give isn't like the peace the world gives. So don't be troubled or afraid. Remember what I told you: I am going away, but I will come back to you again. If you really love me, you will be very happy for me, because now I can go to the Father, who is greater than I am."
John 14:27-28

Sin, fear, uncertainty, doubt, and numerous other forces are at war within us. The peace of God moves into our hearts and lives to restrain these hostile forces and offer comfort in place of conflict. Jesus says he will give us that peace if we are willing to accept it from him.

"For where two or three gather together because they are mine, I am there among them." *Matthew 18:20*

In the body of believers (the church), the sincere agreement of two people in prayer is more powerful than the superficial agreement of thousands, because Christ's Holy Spirit is with them. Two or more believers filled with the Holy Spirit will pray according to God's will, not their own; thus, their requests will be granted.

"And I assure you of this: If anyone acknowledges me publicly here on earth, I, the Son of Man, will openly acknowledge that person in the presence of God's angels." *Luke 12:8*

We acknowledge Jesus when we (1) live a moral, upright, Christ-honoring life, (2) look for opportunities to share our faith with

others, (3) help others in need, (4) take a
stand for justice, (5) love others, (6) acknowledge our loyalty to Christ, and (7) use our
life and resources to carry out his desires
rather than our own.

THE HOPE OF HEAVEN

"Don't be troubled. You trust God, now trust
in me. There are many rooms in my Father's
home, and I am going to prepare a place for
you. If this were not so, I would tell you
plainly. When everything is ready, I will come
and get you, so that you will always be with
me where I am. And you know where I am
going and how to get there." *John 14:1-4*

> Jesus' words show that the way to eternal life,
> though unseen, is secure—as secure as your
> trust in Jesus. He has already prepared the
> way to eternal life. The only issue that may
> still be unsettled is your willingness to believe.

THE HOLY SPIRIT

"I will ask the Father, and he will give you another Counselor, who will never leave you. He is the Holy Spirit, who leads into all truth. The world at large cannot receive him, because it isn't looking for him and doesn't recognize him. But you do, because he lives with you now and later will be in you. No, I will not abandon you as orphans—I will come to you. In just a little while the world will not see me again, but you will. For I will live again, and you will, too." *John 14:16-19*

Jesus was soon going to leave the disciples, but he would remain with them. How could this be? The Counselor—the Spirit of God himself—would come after Jesus was gone to care for and guide the disciples. The Holy Spirit is the very presence of God within us and all believers, helping us live as God wants us to and building Christ's church on earth. By faith we can appropriate the Spirit's power each day.

"But when the Father sends the Counselor as my representative—and by the Counselor I mean the Holy Spirit—he will teach you everything and will remind you of everything I myself have told you." *John 14:26*

Jesus promised the disciples that the Holy Spirit would help them remember what he had been teaching them. This promise ensures the validity of the New Testament. The disciples were eyewitnesses of Jesus' life and teachings, and the Holy Spirit helped them remember without taking away their individual perspectives. The Holy Spirit can help us in the same way. As we study the Bible, we can trust him to plant truth in our mind, convince us of God's will, and remind us when we stray from it.

"But I will send you the Counselor—the Spirit of truth. He will come to you from the Father and will tell you all about me." *John 15:26*

> Once again Jesus offers hope. The Holy Spirit gives strength to endure the unreasonable hatred and evil in our world and the hostility many have toward Christ. This is especially comforting for those facing persecution.

"But it is actually best for you that I go away, because if I don't, the Counselor won't come. If I do go away, he will come because I will send him to you. And when he comes, he will convince the world of its sin, and of God's righteousness, and of the coming judgment." *John 16:7-8*

> Unless Jesus did what he came to do, there would be no Good News. If he did not die, he could not remove our sins; he could not

rise again and defeat death. If he did not go back to the Father, the Holy Spirit would not come. Christ's presence on earth was limited to one place at a time. His leaving meant he could be present to the whole world through the Holy Spirit.

"When the Spirit of truth comes, he will guide you into all truth. He will not be presenting his own ideas; he will be telling you what he has heard. He will tell you about the future. He will bring me glory by revealing to you whatever he receives from me. All that the Father has is mine; this is what I mean when I say that the Spirit will reveal to you whatever he receives from me." *John 16:13-15*

The truth into which the Holy Spirit guides us is the truth about Christ. The Spirit also helps us to discern right from wrong through patient practice.

THE RETURN OF JESUS

"And then at last, the sign of the coming of the Son of Man will appear in the heavens, and there will be deep mourning among all the nations of the earth. And they will see the Son of Man arrive on the clouds of heaven with power and great glory. And he will send forth his angels with the sound of a mighty trumpet blast, and they will gather together his chosen ones from the farthest ends of the earth and heaven." *Matthew 24:30-31*

The nations of the earth will mourn because unbelievers will suddenly realize that they have chosen the wrong side. Everything they have scoffed about will be happening, and it will be too late for them.

"Heaven and earth will disappear, but my words will remain forever.

"However, no one knows the day or the hour when these things will happen, not even the angels in heaven or the Son himself. Only the Father knows.

"When the Son of Man returns, it will be like it was in Noah's day. In those days before the Flood, the people were enjoying banquets and parties and weddings right up to the time Noah entered his boat. People didn't realize what was going to happen until the Flood came and swept them all away. That is the way it will be when the Son of Man comes.

"Two men will be working together in the field; one will be taken, the other left. Two women will be grinding flour at the mill; one will be taken, the other left. So be prepared, because you don't know what day your Lord is coming.

"Know this: A homeowner who knew exactly when a burglar was coming would stay alert and not permit the house to be broken into. You also must be ready all the time. For the Son of Man will come when least expected." *Matthew 24:35-44*

It is good that we don't know exactly when Christ will return. If we knew the precise date, we might be tempted to be lazy in our work for Christ. Christ's second coming will be swift and sudden. There will be no opportunity for last-minute repentance or bargaining. The choice we have already made will determine our eternal destiny.

"Be dressed for service and well prepared, as though you were waiting for your master to return from the wedding feast. Then you will be ready to open the door and let him in the moment he arrives and knocks. There will be special favor for those who are ready and waiting for his return. I tell you, he himself will seat them, put on an apron, and serve them as they sit and eat! He may come in the middle of the night or just before dawn. But whenever he comes, there will be special favor for his servants who are ready!

"Know this: A homeowner who knew exactly when a burglar was coming would not permit the house to be broken into. You must be ready all the time, for the Son of Man will come when least expected."
Luke 12:35-40

> Jesus repeatedly said that he would leave this world but would return at some future time. He also said that a kingdom is being prepared for his followers. Many Greeks envisioned this as a heavenly, idealized spiritual kingdom. Jews— like Isaiah and John, the writer of Revelation—saw it as a restored earthly kingdom.

"See, I am coming soon, and my reward is with me, to repay all according to their deeds. I am the Alpha and the Omega, the First and the Last, the Beginning and the End.

"I, Jesus, have sent my angel to give you this message for the churches. I am both

the source of David and the heir to his throne. I am the bright morning star."
Revelation 22:12-13, 16

Jesus is both David's "source" and "heir."
Jesus, who is one with the Creator of all,
existed long before David. As a human, however, he was one of David's direct descendants. As the Messiah, he is the "bright
morning star," the light of salvation to all.

GOD'S LOVE

"For God so loved the world that he gave his only Son, so that everyone who believes in him will not perish but have eternal life. God did not send his Son into the world to condemn it, but to save it." *John 3:16-17*

The message of the Good News comes to a focus in these verses. Here God sets the pattern of true love, the basis for all love relationships: When you love someone dearly, you are willing to give freely to the point of self-sacrifice. God paid dearly with the life of his Son, the highest price he could pay. Jesus accepted our punishment, paid the price for our sins, and then offered us the new life that he had bought for us. When we share the Good News with others, our love must be like Jesus'— willingly giving up our own comfort and security so that others might join us in receiving God's love.

"I have loved you even as the Father has loved me. Remain in my love. When you obey me, you remain in my love, just as I obey my Father and remain in his love. I have told you this so that you will be filled with my joy. Yes, your joy will overflow!"
John 15:9-11

When things are going well, we feel elated. When hardships come, we sink into depression. But true joy transcends the rolling waves of circumstance. Joy comes from a consistent relationship with Jesus Christ. When our life is intertwined with his, he will help us walk through adversity without sinking into debilitating lows and manage prosperity without moving into deceptive highs.

The joy of living with Jesus Christ daily will keep us levelheaded, no matter how high or low our circumstances.

"For even I, the Son of Man, came here not to be served but to serve others, and to give my life as a ransom for many." *Mark 10:45*

This verse reveals not only the motive for Jesus' ministry but also the basis for our salvation. A ransom was the price paid to release a slave. Jesus paid a ransom for us because we could not pay it ourselves. His death released all of us from our slavery to sin. The disciples thought Jesus' life and power would save them from Rome; Jesus said his *death* would save them from sin, an even greater slavery than Rome's.

"Love your enemies! Do good to them! Lend to them! And don't be concerned that they might not repay. Then your reward from heaven will be very great, and you will truly be acting as children of the Most High, for he is kind to the

unthankful and to those who are wicked.
You must be compassionate, just as your
Father is compassionate." *Luke 6:35-36*

> Love means action. One way to put love
> to work is to take the initiative in meeting
> specific needs. This is easy to do with people
> who love us, people whom we trust; but
> love means doing this even to those who
> dislike us or hurt us. The money we give
> others should be a gift, not a high-interest
> loan that will put a burden on them. Give
> as though you are giving to God.

LOVING GOD

"Those who obey my commandments are the ones who love me. And because they love me, my Father will love them, and I will love them. And I will reveal myself to each one of them." *John 14:21*

> Jesus said that his followers show their love for him by obeying him. Love is more than lovely words; it is commitment and conduct. If you love Christ, then prove it by obeying what he says in his Word.

"If you love your father or mother more than you love me, you are not worthy of being mine; or if you love your son or daughter more than me, you are not worthy of being mine." *Matthew 10:37*

> Christ calls us to a higher mission than to find comfort and tranquility in this life. Love of family is a law of God, but even this love can be self-serving and used as an excuse not to serve God or do his work.

"'You must love the Lord your God with all your heart, all your soul, and all your mind.' This is the first and greatest commandment. A second is equally important: 'Love your neighbor as yourself.' All the other commandments and all the demands of the prophets are based on these two commandments." *Matthew 22:37-40*

> When a Pharisee asked Jesus to identify the most important law, Jesus quoted from Deuteronomy 6:5 and Leviticus 19:18. By fulfilling these two commands, a person keeps all the others. They summarize the Ten Commandments and the other Old Testament moral laws.

"Look at this woman kneeling here. When I entered your home, you didn't offer me water to wash the dust from my feet, but she has washed them with her tears and wiped them with her hair. You didn't give me a kiss of greeting, but she has kissed my feet again and again from the time I first came in. You neglected the courtesy of olive oil to anoint my head, but she has anointed my feet with rare perfume. I tell you, her sins—and they are many—have been forgiven, so she has shown me much love. But a person who is forgiven little shows only little love." *Luke 7:44-47*

Overflowing love is the natural response to forgiveness and the appropriate consequence of faith. But only those who realize the depth of their sin can appreciate the complete forgiveness God offers them. Jesus has rescued all of his followers, whether they were once extremely wicked or conventionally good, from eternal death. Do you appreciate the wideness of God's mercy? Are you grateful for his forgiveness?

99

LOVING OTHERS

"So now I am giving you a new commandment: Love each other. Just as I have loved
you, you should love each other. Your love
for one another will prove to the world that
you are my disciples." *John 13:34-35*

> Jesus says that our Christlike love will show
> that we are his disciples. Do people see
> petty bickering, jealousy, and division in your
> church? Or do they know you are Jesus'
> followers by your love for one another?

"I command you to love each other in the
same way that I love you. And here is how

to measure it—the greatest love is shown when people lay down their lives for their friends. You are my friends if you obey me."
John 15:12-14

> We are to love each other as Jesus loved us, and he loved us enough to give his life for us. We may not have to die for someone, but there are other ways to practice sacrificial love: listening, helping, encouraging, giving. Think of someone in particular who needs this kind of love today. Give all the love you can, and then try to give a little more.

"I command you to love each other. When the world hates you, remember it hated me before it hated you. The world would love you if you belonged to it, but you don't. I chose you to come out of the world, and so it hates you." *John 15:17-19*

> Christians will get plenty of hatred from the world; from each other we need love and support. Do you allow small problems to get in the way of loving other believers?

Jesus commands that you love them, and
he will give you the strength to do it.

"You have heard that the law of Moses
says, 'Love your neighbor' and hate your
enemy. But I say, love your enemies! Pray
for those who persecute you! In that way,
you will be acting as true children of your
Father in heaven. For he gives his sunlight
to both the evil and the good, and he sends
rain on the just and on the unjust, too."
Matthew 5:43-45

By telling us not to retaliate, Jesus keeps us
from taking the law into our own hands. By
loving and praying for our enemies, we can
overcome evil with good.

"But if you are willing to listen, I say, love
your enemies. Do good to those who hate
you. Pray for the happiness of those who
curse you. Pray for those who hurt you. If
someone slaps you on one cheek, turn the
other cheek. If someone demands your
coat, offer your shirt also. Give what you

have to anyone who asks you for it; and when things are taken away from you, don't try to get them back. Do for others as you would like them to do for you." *Luke 6:27-31*

The Jews despised the Romans because they oppressed God's people, but Jesus told the people to love these enemies. Such words turned many away from Christ. But Jesus wasn't talking about having affection for enemies; he was talking about an act of the will. You can't "fall into" this kind of love—it takes conscious effort. Loving our enemies means acting in their best interests. We can pray for them, and we can think of ways to help them. Jesus loved the whole world, even though the world was in rebellion against God. Jesus asks us to follow his example by loving our enemies. Grant your enemies the same respect and rights that you desire for yourself.

"Do you think you deserve credit merely for loving those who love you? Even the sin-

ners do that! And if you do good only to
those who do good to you, is that so wonderful? Even sinners do that much! And if
you lend money only to those who can
repay you, what good is that? Even sinners
will lend to their own kind for a full return."
Luke 6:32-34

> Love means action. One way to put love to
> work is to take the initiative in meeting spe-
> cific needs. This is easy to do with people
> whom we trust; but love means doing this
> even to those who dislike us or hurt us. The
> money we give others should be a gift, not a
> high-interest loan that will put a burden on
> them. Give as though you are giving to God.

"A Jewish man was traveling on a trip from
Jerusalem to Jericho, and he was attacked by
bandits. They stripped him of his clothes
and money, beat him up, and left him half
dead beside the road.

"By chance a Jewish priest came along;
but when he saw the man lying there, he
crossed to the other side of the road and

passed him by. A Temple assistant walked over and looked at him lying there, but he also passed by on the other side.

"Then a despised Samaritan came along, and when he saw the man, he felt deep pity. Kneeling beside him, the Samaritan soothed his wounds with medicine and bandaged them. Then he put the man on his own donkey and took him to an inn, where he took care of him. The next day he handed the innkeeper two pieces of silver and told him to take care of the man. 'If his bill runs higher than that,' he said, 'I'll pay the difference the next time I am here.'

"Now which of these three would you say was a neighbor to the man who was attacked by bandits?" Jesus asked.

The man replied, "The one who showed him mercy."

Then Jesus said, "Yes, now go and do the same." *Luke 10:30-37*

There was deep hatred between Jews and Samaritans. The Jews saw themselves as pure descendants of Abraham, while the Samaritans were a mixed race produced when Jews from the northern kingdom intermarried with other peoples after Israel's exile. To this legal expert, the person least likely to act correctly would be the Samaritan. In fact, he could not bear to say the word *Samaritan* in answer to Jesus' question. This expert's attitude betrayed his lack of the very thing that he had earlier said the law commanded—love.

Forgiveness

GOD'S FORGIVENESS

"If a shepherd has one hundred sheep, and
one wanders away and is lost, what will he
do? Won't he leave the ninety-nine others
and go out into the hills to search for the
lost one? And if he finds it, he will surely
rejoice over it more than over the ninety-
nine that didn't wander away! In the same
way, it is not my heavenly Father's will that
even one of these little ones should perish."
Matthew 18:12-14

Just as a shepherd is concerned enough
about one lost sheep to go search the hills

for it, so God is concerned about every human being he has created. If you come in contact with people in your neighborhood who need Christ, steer them toward him by your example, your words, and your acts of kindness.

"Or suppose a woman has ten valuable silver coins and loses one. Won't she light a lamp and look in every corner of the house and sweep every nook and cranny until she finds it? And when she finds it, she will call in her friends and neighbors to rejoice with her because she has found her lost coin. In the same way, there is joy in the presence of God's angels when even one sinner repents."
Luke 15:8-10

Palestinian women received ten silver coins as a wedding gift. Besides their monetary value, these coins held sentimental value like that of a wedding ring, and to lose one would be extremely distressing. Just as a woman would rejoice at finding her lost coin or ring, so the angels rejoice over a repen-

tant sinner. Each individual is precious to
God. He grieves over every loss and rejoices
whenever one of his children is found and
brought into the Kingdom. Perhaps we
would have more joy in our churches if we
shared Jesus' love and concern for the lost.

"A man had two sons. The younger son told
his father, 'I want my share of your estate
now, instead of waiting until you die.' So his
father agreed to divide his wealth between
his sons.

"A few days later this younger son packed all
his belongings and took a trip to a distant
land, and there he wasted all his money on
wild living. About the time his money ran
out, a great famine swept over the land, and
he began to starve. He persuaded a local
farmer to hire him to feed his pigs. The boy
became so hungry that even the pods he was
feeding the pigs looked good to him. But no
one gave him anything.

"When he finally came to his senses, he
said to himself, 'At home even the hired men

have food enough to spare, and here I am, dying of hunger! I will go home to my father and say, "Father, I have sinned against both heaven and you, and I am no longer worthy of being called your son. Please take me on as a hired man."'

"So he returned home to his father. And while he was still a long distance away, his father saw him coming. Filled with love and compassion, he ran to his son, embraced him, and kissed him. His son said to him, 'Father, I have sinned against both heaven and you, and I am no longer worthy of being called your son.'

"But his father said to the servants, 'Quick! Bring the finest robe in the house and put it on him. Get a ring for his finger, and sandals for his feet. And kill the calf we have been fattening in the pen. We must celebrate with a feast, for this son of mine was dead and has now returned to life. He was lost, but now he is found.' So the party began.

"Meanwhile, the older son was in the fields working. When he returned home, he heard music and dancing in the house, and he asked one of the servants what was going on. 'Your brother is back,' he was told, 'and your father has killed the calf we were fattening and has prepared a great feast. We are celebrating because of his safe return.'

"The older brother was angry and wouldn't go in. His father came out and begged him, but he replied, 'All these years I've worked hard for you and never once refused to do a single thing you told me to. And in all that time you never gave me even one young goat for a feast with my friends. Yet when this son of yours comes back after squandering your money on prostitutes, you celebrate by killing the finest calf we have.'

"His father said to him, 'Look, dear son, you and I are very close, and everything I have is yours. We had to celebrate this happy day. For your brother was dead and has come back to life! He was lost, but now he is found!'"

Luke 15:11-32

In this story, the father watched and waited. He was dealing with a human being with a will of his own, but he was ready to greet his son if he returned. In the same way, God's love is constant and patient and welcoming. He will search for us and give us opportunities to respond, but he will not force us to come to him. Like the father in this story, God waits patiently for us to come to our senses.

FORGIVING OTHERS

"If you forgive those who sin against you,
your heavenly Father will forgive you. But
if you refuse to forgive others, your Father
will not forgive your sins."   *Matthew 6:14-15*

Jesus gives a startling warning about forgiveness: If we refuse to forgive others, God will
also refuse to forgive us. Why? Because
when we don't forgive others, we are deny-
ing our common ground as sinners in need
of God's forgiveness. God's forgiveness of
our sin is not the direct result of our forgiving others, but it is based on our realizing

what forgiveness means. It is easy to ask God for forgiveness but difficult to grant it to others. Whenever we ask God to forgive us for sin, we should ask, "Have I forgiven the people who have wronged me?"

"The Kingdom of Heaven can be compared to a king who decided to bring his accounts up to date with servants who had borrowed money from him. In the process, one of his debtors was brought in who owed him millions of dollars. He couldn't pay, so the king ordered that he, his wife, his children, and everything he had be sold to pay the debt. But the man fell down before the king and begged him, 'Oh, sir, be patient with me, and I will pay it all.' Then the king was filled with pity for him, and he released him and forgave his debt.

"But when the man left the king, he went to a fellow servant who owed him a few thousand dollars. He grabbed him by the throat and demanded instant payment. His fellow servant fell down before him and begged for a little more time. 'Be patient and I will pay it,' he pleaded. But his creditor wouldn't wait. He had the man arrested and jailed until the debt could be paid in full.

"When some of the other servants saw this, they were very upset. They went to the king and told him what had happened. Then the king called in the man he had forgiven and said, 'You evil servant! I forgave you that tremendous debt because you pleaded with me. Shouldn't you have mercy on your fellow servant, just as I had mercy on you?' Then the angry king sent the man to prison until he had paid every penny.

"That's what my heavenly Father will do to you if you refuse to forgive your brothers and sisters in your heart." *Matthew 18:23-35*

> Because God has forgiven all our sins, we should not withhold forgiveness from others. As we realize how completely Christ has forgiven us, it should produce an attitude of forgiveness toward others. When we don't forgive others, we are setting ourselves above Christ's law of love.

Prayer

LEARNING TO PRAY

"Pray like this:

Our Father in heaven,
   may your name be honored.
May your kingdom come soon.
May your will be done here on earth,
   just as it is in heaven.
Give us our food for today,
and forgive us our sins,
   just as we have forgiven those who have
     sinned against us.
And don't let us yield to temptation,
   but deliver us from the evil one."
Matthew 6:9-13

This is often called the Lord's Prayer because Jesus gave it to the disciples. It can be a pattern for our prayers. We should praise God, pray for his work in the world, pray for our daily needs, and pray for help in our daily struggles.

"And now about prayer. When you pray, don't be like the hypocrites who love to pray publicly on street corners and in the synagogues where everyone can see them. I assure you, that is all the reward they will ever get. But when you pray, go away by yourself, shut the door behind you, and pray to your Father secretly. Then your Father, who knows all secrets, will reward you." *Matthew 6:5-6*

Some people, especially the religious leaders, wanted to be seen as "holy," and public prayer was one way to get attention. Jesus saw through their self-righteous acts, however, and taught that the essence of prayer is not public show but private communication with God. There is a place for public prayer, but to pray only where others will notice you indicates that your real audience is not God.

"Two men went to the Temple to pray. One was a Pharisee, and the other was a dishonest tax collector. The proud Pharisee stood by himself and prayed this prayer: 'I thank you, God, that I am not a sinner like everyone else, especially like that tax collector over there! For I never cheat, I don't sin, I don't commit adultery, I fast twice a week, and I give you a tenth of my income.'

"But the tax collector stood at a distance and dared not even lift his eyes to heaven as he prayed. Instead, he beat his chest in sorrow, saying, 'O God, be merciful to me, for I am a sinner.' I tell you, this sinner, not the Pharisee, returned home justified before God. For the proud will be humbled, but the humble will be honored." *Luke 18:10-14*

The Pharisee did not go to the Temple to pray to God but to announce to all how good he was. The tax collector went recognizing his sin and begging for mercy. Self-righteousness is dangerous. It leads to pride, causes a person to despise others, and prevents him or her from learning anything from God. The tax collector's prayer should be our prayer because we all need God's mercy every day. Don't let pride in your achievements cut you off from God.

"When you pray, don't babble on and on as people of other religions do. They think their prayers are answered only by repeating their words again and again. Don't be like them, because your Father knows exactly what you need even before you ask him!"
Matthew 6:7-8

Repeating the same words over and over like a magic incantation is no way to ensure that God will hear your prayer. It's not wrong to come to God many times with the same requests—Jesus encourages *persistent* prayer. But he condemns the shallow repetition of words that are not offered with a sincere heart. We can never pray too much if our prayers are honest and sincere. Before you start to pray, make sure you mean what you say.

PERSISTENCE IN PRAYER

"Keep on asking, and you will be given what you ask for. Keep on looking, and you will find. Keep on knocking, and the door will be opened. For everyone who asks, receives. Everyone who seeks, finds. And the door is opened to everyone who knocks. You parents—if your children ask for a loaf of bread, do you give them a stone instead? Or if they ask for a fish, do you give them a snake? Of course not! If you sinful people know how to give good gifts to your children, how much more will your heavenly Father give good gifts to those who ask him." *Matthew 7:7-11*

Jesus tells us to persist in pursuing God. People often give up after a few halfhearted efforts and conclude that God cannot be found. But knowing God takes faith, focus, and follow-through, and Jesus assures us that we will be rewarded. Don't give up in your efforts to seek God. Continue to ask him for more knowledge, patience, wisdom, love, and understanding. He will give them to you.

"Suppose you went to a friend's house at midnight, wanting to borrow three loaves of bread. You would say to him, 'A friend of mine has just arrived for a visit, and I have nothing for him to eat.' He would call out from his bedroom, 'Don't bother me. The door is locked for the night, and we are all in bed. I can't help you this time.' But I tell you this—though he won't do it as a friend, if you keep knocking long enough, he will get up and give you what you want so his reputation won't be damaged.

"And so I tell you, keep on asking, and you will be given what you ask for. Keep on looking, and you will find. Keep on knocking, and the door will be opened. For everyone who asks, receives. Everyone who seeks, finds. And the door is opened to everyone who knocks." *Luke 11:5-10*

> Persistence, or boldness, in prayer overcomes our insensitivity, not God's. To practice persistence does more to change our heart and mind than his, and it helps us understand and express the intensity of our need. Persistence in prayer helps us recognize God's work.

"There was a judge in a certain city . . . who was a godless man with great contempt for everyone. A widow of that city came to him repeatedly, appealing for justice against someone who had harmed her. The judge ignored her for a while, but eventually she wore him out. 'I fear neither God nor man,' he said to himself, 'but this woman is driving me crazy. I'm going to see that she gets justice, because she is wearing me out with her constant requests!'" *Luke 18:2-5*

If godless judges respond to constant pressure, how much more will a great and loving God respond to us. If we know he loves us, we can believe he will hear our cries for help.

THE RESULTS OF PRAYER

"The truth is, anyone who believes in me
will do the same works I have done, and
even greater works, because I am going to
be with the Father. You can ask for anything
in my name, and I will do it, because the
work of the Son brings glory to the Father.
Yes, ask anything in my name, and I will
do it!" *John 14:12-14*

> When Jesus says we can ask for anything,
> we must remember that our asking must
> be in his name—that is, according to God's
> character and will. God will not grant

requests contrary to his nature or his will, and we cannot use his name as a magic formula to fulfill our selfish desires. If we are sincerely following God and seeking to do his will, then our requests will be in line with what he wants, and he will grant them.

"Then you will ask in my name. I'm not saying I will ask the Father on your behalf, for the Father himself loves you dearly because you love me and believe that I came from God." John 16:26-27

Jesus is talking about a new relationship between the believer and God. Previously, people approached God through priests. After Jesus' resurrection, any believer could approach God directly. A new day had dawned, and now all believers are priests and can talk with God personally and directly. We approach God, not because of our own merit, but because Jesus, our great High Priest, has made us acceptable to God.

"You fathers—if your children ask for a fish, do you give them a snake instead? Or if they ask for an egg, do you give them a scorpion? Of course not! If you sinful people know how to give good gifts to your children, how much more will your heavenly Father give the Holy Spirit to those who ask him." *Luke 11:11-13*

> Even though good fathers make mistakes, they treat their children well. How much better our perfect heavenly Father treats his children! The most important gift he could ever give us is the Holy Spirit, whom he promised to give all believers after his Son's death, resurrection, and return to heaven.

"I also tell you this: If two of you agree down here on earth concerning anything you ask, my Father in heaven will do it for you. For where two or three gather together because they are mine, I am there among them." *Matthew 18:19-20*

> Jesus looked ahead to a new day when he would be present with his followers, not in

body but through his Holy Spirit. In the body of believers (the church), the sincere agreement of two people in prayer is more powerful than the superficial agreement of thousands, because Christ's Holy Spirit is with them. Two or more believers *filled with the Holy Spirit* will pray according to God's will, not their own; thus, their requests will be granted.

THE IMPORTANCE OF FAITH

"I assure you, if you have faith and don't doubt, you can do things like this and much more. You can even say to this mountain, 'May God lift you up and throw you into the sea,' and it will happen. If you believe, you will receive whatever you ask for in prayer." *Matthew 21:21-22*

Many have wondered about Jesus' statement that if we have faith and don't doubt, we can move mountains. Jesus, of course, was not suggesting that his followers use prayer as "magic" to perform capricious mountain-moving acts. Instead, he was making a strong point about the disciples' (and our) lack of faith. What kinds of mountains do you face? Have you talked to God about them? How strong is your faith?

"Have faith in God. I assure you that you can say to this mountain, 'May God lift you up and throw you into the sea,' and your command will be obeyed. All that's required is that you really believe and do not doubt in your heart. Listen to me! You can pray for anything, and if you believe, you will have it. But when you are praying, first forgive anyone you are holding a grudge against, so that your Father in heaven will forgive your sins, too." *Mark 11:22-25*

Jesus, our example, prayed, "Everything is possible for you. . . . Yet I want your will, not mine" (Mark 14:36). Our prayers are often motivated by our own interests and desires. We like to hear that we can have anything. But Jesus prayed with *God's* interests in mind. When we pray, we can express our desires, but we should want his will above ours. Check to see if your prayers focus on your interests or God's.

PRAYERS OF JESUS

"O Father, Lord of heaven and earth,
thank you for hiding the truth from those
who think themselves so wise and clever,
and for revealing it to the childlike. Yes,
Father, it pleased you to do it this way!"
Matthew 11:25-26

> Jesus mentioned two kinds of people in his
> prayer: the "wise and clever"—arrogant in
> their own knowledge—and the "childlike"—
> humbly open to receive the truth of God's
> Word. Are you wise in your own eyes, or do
> you seek the truth in childlike faith, realizing
> that only God holds all the answers?

"Father, may your name be honored. May your Kingdom come soon. Give us our food day by day. And forgive us our sins— just as we forgive those who have sinned against us. And don't let us yield to temptation." *Luke 11:2-4*

> Notice the order in this prayer. First Jesus praised God; then he made his requests. Praising God first focuses our thoughts on his greatness and glory before we begin our requests. Too often our prayers are more like shopping lists than conversations.

"Father, the time has come. Glorify your Son so he can give glory back to you. For you have given him authority over everyone in all the earth. He gives eternal life to each one you have given him. And this is the way to have eternal life—to know you, the only true God, and Jesus Christ, the one you sent to earth. I brought glory to you here on earth by doing everything you told me to do. And now, Father, bring me into the glory we shared before the world began.

"I have told these men about you. They were in the world, but then you gave them to me. Actually, they were always yours, and you gave them to me; and they have kept your word. Now they know that everything I have is a gift from you, for I have passed on to them the words you gave me; and they accepted them and know that I came from you, and they believe you sent me.

"My prayer is not for the world, but for those you have given me, because they belong to you. And all of them, since they are mine, belong to you; and you have given them back to me, so they are my glory! Now I am departing the world; I am leaving them behind and coming to you. Holy Father, keep them and care for them—all those you have given me— so that they will be united just as we are. During my time here, I have kept them safe. I guarded them so that not one was lost, except the one headed for destruction, as the Scriptures foretold.

"And now I am coming to you. I have

told them many things while I was with them so they would be filled with my joy. I have given them your word. And the world hates them because they do not belong to the world, just as I do not. I'm not asking you to take them out of the world, but to keep them safe from the evil one. They are not part of this world any more than I am. Make them pure and holy by teaching them your words of truth. As you sent me into the world, I am sending them into the world. And I give myself entirely to you so they also might be entirely yours.

"I am praying not only for these disciples but also for all who will ever believe in me because of their testimony. My prayer for all of them is that they will be one, just as you and I are one, Father—that just as you are in me and I am in you, so they will be in us, and the world will believe you sent me.

"I have given them the glory you gave me, so that they may be one, as we are—I in them and you in me, all being perfected into one. Then the world will know that

you sent me and will understand that you
love them as much as you love me. Father,
I want these whom you've given me to be
with me, so they can see my glory. You gave
me the glory because you loved me even
before the world began!

"O righteous Father, the world doesn't
know you, but I do; and these disciples
know you sent me. And I have revealed you
to them and will keep on revealing you. I
will do this so that your love for me may
be in them and I in them." *John 17:1-26*

From this prayer we learn that the world
is a tremendous battleground where the
forces under Satan's power and those under
God's authority are at war. Satan and his
forces are motivated by bitter hatred for
Christ and his forces. Jesus prayed for his
disciples, including those of us who follow
him today. He prayed that God would keep
his chosen believers safe from Satan's power,
setting them apart and making them pure
and holy, uniting them through his truth.

"My Father! If it is possible, let this cup of suffering be taken away from me. Yet I want your will, not mine. . . . My Father! If this cup cannot be taken away until I drink it, your will be done." *Matthew 26:39, 42*

> Jesus was not rebelling against his Father's will when he asked that the cup of suffering and separation be taken away. In fact, he reaffirmed his desire to do God's will by saying, "Yet I want your will, not mine." Jesus' prayer reveals to us his terrible suffering. His agony was worse than death because he paid for all sin by being separated from God. The sinless Son of God took our sins upon himself to save us from suffering and separation.

"Eli, Eli, lema sabachthani? . . . My God, my God, why have you forsaken me?"
Matthew 27:46

> Jesus was not questioning God; he was quoting the first line of Psalm 22—a deep expression of the anguish he felt when he took on the sins of the world, which separated him from his Father. This was what Jesus dreaded

as he prayed to God in the garden to take the cup from him. The physical agony was horrible, but even worse was the period of spiritual separation from God. Jesus suffered this double death so we would never have to experience eternal separation from God.

"Father, forgive these people, because they don't know what they are doing."
Luke 23:34

Jesus asked God to forgive the people who were putting him to death—Jewish leaders, Roman politicians and soldiers, bystanders— and God answered that prayer by opening up the way of salvation even to Jesus' murderers. The Roman officer and soldiers who witnessed the Crucifixion said, "Truly, this was the Son of God!" (Matthew 27:54). Soon many priests were converted to the Christian faith. Because we are all sinners, we all played a part in putting Jesus to death. The good news is that God is gracious. He will forgive us and give us new life through his Son.

"Father, I entrust my spirit into your hands!"
Luke 23:46

> It is believed that this prayer, Jesus' final
> words on the cross, is part of David's Psalm
> 31. Regardless of what is going on in our life,
> we need to entrust ourselves into our
> Father's hands.

The Kingdom of God

NATURE OF THE KINGDOM

"The Kingdom of Heaven is like a mustard seed planted in a field. It is the smallest of all seeds, but it becomes the largest of garden plants and grows into a tree where birds can come and find shelter in its branches." *Matthew 13:31-32*

> The mustard seed was the smallest seed a farmer used. Jesus used this parable to show that the Kingdom has small beginnings but will grow and produce great results.

"The Kingdom of Heaven is like yeast used by a woman making bread. Even though

she used a large amount of flour, the yeast
permeated every part of the dough."
Matthew 13:33

> In other Bible passages, yeast is used as a
> symbol of evil or uncleanness. Here it is a
> positive symbol of growth. Although yeast
> looks like a minor ingredient, it permeates
> the whole loaf. Although the Kingdom began
> small and was nearly invisible, it would soon
> grow and have a great impact on the world.

"The Kingdom of Heaven is like a treasure
that a man discovered hidden in a field. In
his excitement, he hid it again and sold everything he owned to get enough money to buy
the field—and to get the treasure, too!"
Matthew 13:44

> The Kingdom of Heaven is more valuable
> than anything else we can have, and a per-
> son must be willing to give up everything to
> obtain it. The man who discovered the trea-
> sure in the field stumbled upon it by accident
> but knew its value when he found it. So he
> sold everything he had to purchase the field.

"The Kingdom of Heaven is like a pearl merchant on the lookout for choice pearls. When he discovered a pearl of great value, he sold everything he owned and bought it!" *Matthew 13:45-46*

> The merchant was earnestly searching for the pearl of great value, and when he found it, he sold everything he had to purchase it.

"The Kingdom of God isn't ushered in with visible signs. You won't be able to say, 'Here it is!' or 'It's over there!' For the Kingdom of God is among you." *Luke 17:20-21*

> The Kingdom of God is not like an earthly kingdom with geographical boundaries. Instead, it begins with the work of God's Spirit in people's lives and in relationships. We must resist looking to institutions or programs for evidence of the progress of God's Kingdom. We should look for what God is doing in people's hearts.

ENTERING THE KINGDOM

"You can enter God's Kingdom only through the narrow gate. The highway to hell is broad, and its gate is wide for the many who choose the easy way. But the gateway to life is small, and the road is narrow, and only a few ever find it." *Matthew 7:13-14*

The gate that leads to eternal life is called "narrow." This does not mean that it is difficult to become a Christian but that there is only *one* way to eternal life with God and only a few decide to walk that road. Believing in Jesus is the only way to heaven, because he alone died for our sins and made us right before God. Living his way may not be popular, but it is true and right. Thank God there is one way!

"Not all people who sound religious are really godly. They may refer to me as 'Lord,' but they still won't enter the Kingdom of Heaven. The decisive issue is whether they obey my Father in heaven. On judgment day many will tell me, 'Lord, Lord, we prophesied in your name and cast out demons in your name and performed many miracles in your name.' But I will reply, 'I never knew you. Go away; the things you did were unauthorized.'" *Matthew 7:21-23*

Jesus exposed those people who sounded religious but had no personal relationship with him. On judgment day only our relationship with Christ—our acceptance of him as Savior and our obedience to him—will matter. Many people think that if they are good people and say religious things, they will be rewarded with eternal life. In reality, faith in Christ is what will count at the judgment.

"If anyone acknowledges me publicly here on earth, I will openly acknowledge that person before my Father in heaven. But if anyone denies me here on earth, I will deny that person before my Father in heaven."
Matthew 10:32-33

> We can reject Jesus now and be rejected by him at his second coming, or we can accept him now and be accepted by him when he comes again. Rejecting Christ may help us escape shame for the time being, but it will guarantee an eternity of shame later.

"Let the children come to me. Don't stop them! For the Kingdom of God belongs to such as these. I assure you, anyone who doesn't have their kind of faith will never get into the Kingdom of God." *Mark 10:14-15*

> To feel secure, all children need is a loving look and gentle touch from someone who cares. They believe us because they trust us. Jesus said that people should trust in him with this kind of childlike faith. We do not have to understand all the mysteries

of the universe; it should be enough to know that God loves us and provides forgiveness for our sin. This doesn't mean that we should be childish or immature but that we should trust God with a child's simplicity and receptivity.

"How hard it is for rich people to get into the Kingdom of God! . . . Dear children, it is very hard to get into the Kingdom of God. It is easier for a camel to go through the eye of a needle than for a rich person to enter the Kingdom of God! . . .

"Humanly speaking, it is impossible. But not with God. Everything is possible with God." *Mark 10:23-25, 27*

Jesus said that it was very difficult for the rich to enter the Kingdom of God because the rich, having their basic physical needs met, often become self-reliant. When they feel empty, they buy something new to try to fill the void that only God can fill. Their abundance and self-sufficiency become their deficiency. The person who has everything

on earth can still lack what is most important—eternal life.

"The truth is, no one can enter the Kingdom of God without being born of water
and the Spirit. Humans can reproduce only
human life, but the Holy Spirit gives new
life from heaven. So don't be surprised at
my statement that you must be born again.
Just as you can hear the wind but can't tell
where it comes from or where it is going,
so you can't explain how people are born
of the Spirit." *John 3:5-8*

"Of water and the Spirit" could refer to
(1) the contrast between physical birth
(water) and spiritual birth (Spirit) or to
(2) the regeneration by the Spirit and the
sign of that rebirth by Christian baptism.
The water may also represent the cleans-
ing action of God's Holy Spirit. Jesus was
explaining the importance of a spiritual
rebirth, saying that people don't enter the
Kingdom by living a better life but by being
spiritually reborn.

Other Teachings of Jesus

DON'T CRITICIZE OTHERS

"Stop judging others, and you will not be
judged. Stop criticizing others, or it will all
come back on you. If you forgive others,
you will be forgiven. If you give, you will
receive. Your gift will return to you in full
measure, pressed down, shaken together
to make room for more, and running over.
Whatever measure you use in giving— large
or small—it will be used to measure what
is given back to you." *Luke 6:37-38*

A forgiving spirit demonstrates that a person
has received God's forgiveness. Jesus uses the
picture of measuring grain in a basket to

ensure the full amount. If we are critical rather than compassionate, we will also receive criticism. If we treat others generously, graciously, and compassionately, however, these qualities will come back to us in full measure. We are to love others, not judge them.

"And why worry about a speck in your friend's eye when you have a log in your own? How can you think of saying, 'Friend, let me help you get rid of that speck in your eye,' when you can't see past the log in your own eye? Hypocrite! First get rid of the log from your own eye; then perhaps you will see well enough to deal with the speck in your friend's eye!" *Luke 6:41-42*

Jesus doesn't mean we should ignore wrongdoing, but we should not be so worried about others' sins that we overlook our own. We often rationalize our sins by pointing out the same mistakes in others. What kinds of specks in others' eyes are the easiest for you to criticize? Remember your own "logs" when you feel like criticizing, and you may find that you have less to say.

DON'T WORRY

"So I tell you, don't worry about everyday life—whether you have enough food, drink, and clothes. Doesn't life consist of more than food and clothing? Look at the birds. They don't need to plant or harvest or put food in barns because your heavenly Father feeds them. And you are far more valuable to him than they are. Can all your worries add a single moment to your life? Of course not.

"And why worry about your clothes? Look at the lilies and how they grow. They don't work or make their clothing, yet Solomon in all his glory was not dressed as beautifully as they are. And if God cares so wonderfully for flowers that are here today and gone tomorrow, won't he more surely care for you? You have so little faith!" *Matthew 6:25-30*

> Jesus tells us not to worry about those needs that God promises to supply. Worry may (1) damage your health, (2) disrupt your productivity, (3) negatively affect the way you treat others, and (4) reduce your ability to trust in God. How many ill effects of worry are you experiencing? The difference between worry and genuine concern is clear: Worry immobilizes, but concern moves you to action.

"So don't worry about tomorrow, for tomorrow will bring its own worries. Today's trouble is enough for today." *Matthew 6:34*

> Planning for tomorrow is time well spent; worrying about tomorrow is time wasted. Worriers are consumed by fear and find it difficult to trust God. They let their plans interfere with their relationship with God. Don't let worries about tomorrow affect your relationship with God today.

"These things dominate the thoughts of most people, but your Father already knows your needs. He will give you all you need from day to day if you make the Kingdom of God your primary concern."
Luke 12:30-31

> Making the Kingdom of God your primary concern means making Jesus the Lord and King of your life. He must control every area—your work, play, plans, and relationships. Is the Kingdom only one of your many concerns, or is it central to all you do? Are you holding back any areas of your life from God's control? As Lord and Creator, he wants to help provide what you need as well as guide you in using what he provides.

"Don't be afraid of those who want to kill you. They can only kill your body; they cannot touch your soul. Fear only God, who can destroy both soul and body in hell. Not even a sparrow, worth only half a penny, can fall to the ground without your Father knowing it. And the very hairs on your

head are all numbered. So don't be afraid;
you are more valuable to him than a whole
flock of sparrows." *Matthew 10:28-31*

Jesus said that God is aware of everything
that happens even to sparrows, and you
are far more valuable to him than they are.
You are so valuable that God sent his only
Son to die for you. Because God places
such value on you, you need never fear
personal threats or difficult trials. These can't
shake God's love or dislodge his Spirit from
within you.

But this doesn't mean that God will take
away all your troubles. The real test of
strength is how well something holds up
under the wear, tear, and stress of everyday
life. Those who stand up for Christ in spite
of their troubles will receive great rewards.

ETERNAL LIFE

"This is the way to have eternal life—to know you, the only true God, and Jesus Christ, the one you sent to earth." *John 17:3*

> How do we get eternal life? Jesus tells us clearly here—by knowing God the Father himself through his Son, Jesus Christ. Eternal life requires entering into a personal relationship with God in Jesus Christ. When we admit our sin and turn away from it, Christ's love lives in us through the Holy Spirit.

"I assure you, those who listen to my message and believe in God who sent me have eternal life. They will never be condemned for their sins, but they have already passed from death into life." *John 5:24*

> Eternal life—living forever with God—begins when you accept Jesus Christ as Savior. At that moment, new life begins in you. It is a completed transaction. You will still face physical death, but when Christ returns, your body will be resurrected to live forever with him in heaven.

"For it is my Father's will that all who see his Son and believe in him should have eternal life—that I should raise them at the last day." *John 6:40*

> Those who put their faith in Christ will be resurrected from physical death to eternal life with God when Christ comes again.

"I assure you, anyone who believes in me already has eternal life. Yes, I am the bread of life! Your ancestors ate manna in the wilderness, but they all died. However, the bread from heaven gives eternal life to everyone who eats it. I am the living bread that came down out of heaven. Anyone who eats this bread will live forever; this bread is my flesh, offered so the world may live." *John 6:47-51*

> Here Jesus refers to the manna that God had given their ancestors in the wilderness during Moses' time. This bread was physical and temporal. The people ate it, and it sustained them for a day. But they had to get more bread every day, and this bread could not keep them from dying. Jesus, who is much greater than Moses, offers himself as the spiritual bread from heaven that satisfies completely and leads to eternal life.

HEARING AND OBEYING

"Not all people who sound religious are
really godly. They may refer to me as 'Lord,'
but they still won't enter the Kingdom of
Heaven. The decisive issue is whether they
obey my Father in heaven. On judgment day
many will tell me, 'Lord, Lord, we prophesied
in your name and cast out demons in your
name and performed many miracles in your
name.' But I will reply, 'I never knew you. Go
away; the things you did were unauthorized.'"
Matthew 7:21-23

It is important to listen to what God's Word
says, but it is much more important to obey

it and to *do* what it says. Do you put your faith into action?

"Anyone who listens to my teaching and obeys me is wise, like a person who builds a house on solid rock. Though the rain comes in torrents and the floodwaters rise and the winds beat against that house, it won't collapse, because it is built on rock. But anyone who hears my teaching and ignores it is foolish, like a person who builds a house on sand. When the rains and floods come and the winds beat against that house, it will fall with a mighty crash." *Matthew 7:24-27*

> To build "on solid rock" means to be a hearing, responding disciple, not a phony, superficial one. Obedience becomes the solid foundation to weather the storms of life.

"But what do you think about this? A man with two sons told the older boy, 'Son, go out and work in the vineyard today.' The son answered, 'No, I won't go,' but later he

changed his mind and went anyway. Then
the father told the other son, 'You go,' and
he said, 'Yes, sir, I will.' But he didn't go.
Which of the two was obeying his father?"
Matthew 21:28-31

> The son who said he would obey and then
> didn't represented the people of Israel in
> Jesus' day. They said they wanted to do
> God's will, but they constantly disobeyed
> him. They were phony, just going through
> the motions. It is dangerous to pretend to
> obey God when our heart is far from him,
> because God knows our true intentions.
> Our actions must match our words.

"A farmer went out to plant some seed. As
he scattered it across his field, some seed
fell on a footpath, where it was stepped on,
and the birds came and ate it. Other seed
fell on shallow soil with underlying rock.
This seed began to grow, but soon it with-
ered and died for lack of moisture. Other
seed fell among thorns that shot up and
choked out the tender blades. Still other

seed fell on fertile soil. This seed grew and produced a crop one hundred times as much as had been planted. . . .

"This is the meaning of the story: The seed is God's message. The seed that fell on the hard path represents those who hear the message, but then the Devil comes and steals it away and prevents them from believing and being saved. The rocky soil represents those who hear the message with joy. But like young plants in such soil, their roots don't go very deep. They believe for a while, but they wilt when the hot winds of testing blow. The thorny ground represents those who hear and accept the message, but all too quickly the message is crowded out by the cares and riches and pleasures of this life. And so they never grow into maturity. But the good soil represents honest, good-hearted people who hear God's message, cling to it, and steadily produce a huge harvest." *Luke 8:5-8; 11-15*

"Path" people, like many of the religious leaders in Jesus' time, refused to believe God's message. "Rock" people, like many in the crowd who followed Jesus, believed his message but never got around to doing anything about it. "Thorn" people, overcome by worries and the lure of materialism, left no room in their lives for God. "Good soil" people, in contrast to all the other groups, followed Jesus no matter what the cost. Which type of soil are you?

JESUS AND THE LAW

"Don't misunderstand why I have come.
I did not come to abolish the law of
Moses or the writings of the prophets. No,
I came to fulfill them. I assure you, until
heaven and earth disappear, even the
smallest detail of God's law will remain
until its purpose is achieved. So if you
break the smallest commandment and
teach others to do the same, you will be
the least in the Kingdom of Heaven. But
anyone who obeys God's laws and teaches
them will be great in the Kingdom of
Heaven." *Matthew 5:17-19*

Some of those in the crowd were experts at telling others what to do, but they missed the central point of God's laws themselves. Jesus made it clear, however, that obeying God's laws is more important than explaining them. It's much easier to study God's laws and tell others to obey them than to put them into practice. How are you doing at obeying God *yourself*?

"You have heard that the law of Moses says, 'Do not murder. If you commit murder, you are subject to judgment.' But I say, if you are angry with someone, you are subject to judgment! If you say to your friend, 'You idiot,' you are in danger of being brought before the court. And if you curse someone, you are in danger of the fires of hell."
Matthew 5:21-22

When Jesus said, "But I say," he was not doing away with the law or adding his own beliefs. Rather, he was giving a fuller understanding of why God made that law in the first place. For example, Moses said, "Do not

murder" (Exodus 20:13); Jesus taught that
we should not even become angry enough
to murder, for if we do we have already
committed murder in our heart. The Pharisees read this law and, not having literally
murdered anyone, felt that they had obeyed
it. Yet they were so angry with Jesus that
they would soon plot his death, though they
would not do the dirty work themselves.
We miss the intent of God's Word when
we read his rules for living without trying
to understand why he made them. When
do you keep God's rules but close your eyes
to his intent?

"Again, you have heard that the law of
Moses says, 'Do not break your vows; you
must carry out the vows you have made to
the Lord.' But I say, don't make any vows!
If you say, 'By heaven!' it is a sacred vow
because heaven is God's throne. And if you
say, 'By the earth!' it is a sacred vow because
the earth is his footstool. And don't swear,
'By Jerusalem!' for Jerusalem is the city of

the great King. Don't even swear, 'By my head!' for you can't turn one hair white or black. Just say a simple, 'Yes, I will,' or 'No, I won't.' Your word is enough. To strengthen your promise with a vow shows that something is wrong." *Matthew 5:33-37*

> Vows were common, but Jesus told his followers not to use them—their word alone should be enough. Are you known as a person of your word? Truthfulness seems so rare that we feel we must end our statements with "I promise." If we tell the truth all the time, we will have less pressure to back up our words with an oath or promise.

"You have heard that the law of Moses says, 'If an eye is injured, injure the eye of the person who did it. If a tooth gets knocked out, knock out the tooth of the person who did it.' But I say, don't resist an evil person! If you are slapped on the right cheek, turn the other, too. If you are ordered to court and your shirt is taken from you, give your coat, too. If a soldier demands that you carry his gear for a mile, carry it two miles. Give to those who ask, and don't turn away from those who want to borrow." *Matthew 5:38-42*

> To many Jews of Jesus' day, these statements were offensive. Any Messiah who would turn the other cheek was not the military leader they wanted to lead a revolt against Rome. Since they were under Roman oppression, they wanted retaliation against their enemies, whom they hated. But Jesus suggested a new, radical response to injustice: Instead of demanding rights, give them up freely! According to Jesus, it is more important to give justice and mercy than to receive it.

"If you had one sheep, and it fell into a well on the Sabbath, wouldn't you get to work and pull it out? Of course you would. And how much more valuable is a person than a sheep! Yes, it is right to do good on the Sabbath." *Matthew 12:11-12*

The Pharisees placed their laws above human need. They were so concerned about Jesus' breaking one of their rules that they did not care about the man's deformed hand. What is your attitude toward others? If your convictions don't allow you to help certain people, your convictions may not be in tune with God's Word. Don't allow dogma to blind you to human need.

"Haven't you ever read in the Scriptures what King David did when he and his companions were hungry? He went into the house of God (during the days when Abiathar was high priest), ate the special bread reserved for the priests alone, and then gave some to his companions. That was breaking the law, too. . . . The Sabbath was made to benefit people, and not people to benefit the Sabbath. And I, the Son of Man, am master even of the Sabbath!" *Mark 2:25-28*

God created the Sabbath for our benefit, not his own. God derives no benefit from having us rest on the Sabbath, but we are restored both physically and spiritually when we take time to rest and focus on God. For the Pharisees, Sabbath laws had become more important than Sabbath rest. Both David and Jesus understood that the intent of God's law is to promote love for God and others. When we apply a law to other people, we should make sure that we understand its purpose and intent so we don't make harmful or inappropriate judgments.

MARRIAGE AND DIVORCE

"You have heard that the law of Moses says, 'Do not commit adultery.' But I say, anyone who even looks at a woman with lust in his eye has already committed adultery with her in his heart. So if your eye—even if it is your good eye—causes you to lust, gouge it out and throw it away. It is better for you to lose one part of your body than for your whole body to be thrown into hell. And if your hand—even if it is your stronger hand—causes you to sin, cut it off and throw it away. It is better for you to lose one part of your body than for your whole body to be thrown into hell." *Matthew 5:27-30*

> The Old Testament law said that it is wrong for a person to have sex with someone other than his or her spouse. But Jesus said that the *desire* to have sex with someone other than your spouse is mental adultery and thus sin. Jesus emphasized that if the *act* is wrong, then so is the *intention*. To be faithful to your spouse with your body but not your mind is to break the trust so vital to a strong marriage. Jesus is condemning not natural interest in the opposite sex or even healthy sexual desire but the deliberate and repeated filling of one's mind with illicit fantasies.

"You have heard that the law of Moses says, 'A man can divorce his wife by merely giving her a letter of divorce.' But I say that a man who divorces his wife, unless she has been unfaithful, causes her to commit adultery. And anyone who marries a divorced woman commits adultery." *Matthew 5:31-32*

Divorce is as hurtful and destructive today as it was in Jesus' day. God intends marriage to be a lifetime commitment. When entering into marriage, people should never consider divorce an option for solving problems or a way out of a relationship that seems dead. In these verses Jesus is attacking those who purposefully abuse the marriage contract, using divorce to satisfy their lustful desire to marry someone else. Are your actions today helping your marriage grow stronger, or are you tearing it apart?

"Whoever divorces his wife and marries someone else commits adultery against her. And if a woman divorces her husband and remarries, she commits adultery." *Mark 10:11-12*

Don't enter marriage with the option of getting out. Your marriage is more likely to be happy if from the outset you are committed to permanence. Don't be hard-hearted like these Pharisees, but be hard-hearted in your determination, with God's help, to stay together.

"Haven't you read the Scriptures? . . .
They record that from the beginning 'God
made them male and female.' And he said,
'This explains why a man leaves his father
and mother and is joined to his wife, and
the two are united into one.' Since they
are no longer two but one, let no one
separate them, for God has joined them
together. . . .

"Moses permitted divorce as a concession
to your hard-hearted wickedness, but it was
not what God had originally intended. And
I tell you this, a man who divorces his wife
and marries another commits adultery—
unless his wife has been unfaithful."
Matthew 19:4-6, 8-9

In Jesus' time two schools of thought represented two opposing views of divorce. One
group supported divorce for almost any
reason. The other believed that divorce
could be allowed only for marital unfaithful-
ness. This conflict hinged on how each group
interpreted Deuteronomy 24:1-4. In his
answer, however, Jesus focused on marriage

rather than divorce. He pointed out that God intended marriage to be permanent and gave four reasons for the importance of marriage.

MONEY AND POSSESSIONS

"Don't store up treasures here on earth, where they can be eaten by moths and get rusty, and where thieves break in and steal. Store your treasures in heaven, where they will never become moth-eaten or rusty and where they will be safe from thieves. Wherever your treasure is, there your heart and thoughts will also be." *Matthew 6:19-21*

Jesus contrasted heavenly values with earthly values when he explained that our first loyalty should be to those things that do not fade, cannot be stolen or used up,

and never wear out. Storing treasures in
heaven is not limited to tithing but is accomplished by all acts of obedience to God.
There is a sense in which giving our money
to God's work is like investing in heaven.
But we should seek to please God not only
in our giving but also in fulfilling God's pur-
poses in all we do.

"No one can serve two masters. For you will
hate one and love the other, or be devoted
to one and despise the other. You cannot
serve both God and money." *Matthew 6:24*

We should not be fascinated with our possessions, lest *they* possess *us*. This means we
may have to do some cutting back if our
possessions are becoming too important to
us. Jesus is calling for a decision that allows
us to live contentedly with whatever we
have because we have chosen what is eternal and lasting.

"So don't worry about having enough food
or drink or clothing. Why be like the

190

pagans who are so deeply concerned about these things? Your heavenly Father already knows all your needs, and he will give you all you need from day to day if you live for him and make the Kingdom of God your primary concern." *Matthew 6:31-33*

To "make the Kingdom of God your primary concern" means to put God first in your life, to fill your thoughts with his desires, to pattern your character after his, and to serve and obey him in everything. What is really important to you? People, objects, goals, and desires all compete for priority. Any of these can quickly bump God out of first place if you don't actively choose to give him first place in *every* area of your life.

"I tell you the truth, it is very hard for a rich person to get into the Kingdom of Heaven. I say it again—it is easier for a camel to go through the eye of a needle than for a rich person to enter the Kingdom of God!" *Matthew 19:23-24*

Because it is impossible for a camel to go
through the eye of a needle, it appears
impossible for a rich person to get into the
Kingdom of Heaven. Jesus explained, however, that "with God everything is possible"
(Matthew 19:26). Even rich people can
enter the Kingdom if God brings them in.
Faith in Christ, not in self or riches, is what
counts. On what are you counting for salvation?

"What sorrows await you who are rich,
for you have your only happiness now.
What sorrows await you who are satisfied
and prosperous now, for a time of awful
hunger is before you. What sorrows await
you who laugh carelessly, for your laugh-
ing will turn to mourning and sorrow."
Luke 6:24-25

If you are trying to find fulfillment only
through riches, wealth may be the only
reward you will ever get—and it does not
last. We should not seek comfort now at
the expense of eternal life.

"A rich man had a fertile farm that produced fine crops. In fact, his barns were full to overflowing. So he said, 'I know! I'll tear down my barns and build bigger ones. Then I'll have room enough to store everything. And I'll sit back and say to myself, My friend, you have enough stored away for years to come. Now take it easy! Eat, drink, and be merry!'

"But God said to him, 'You fool! You will die this very night. Then who will get it all?'

"Yes, a person is a fool to store up earthly wealth but not have a rich relationship with God." *Luke 12:16-21*

> The rich man in Jesus' story died before he could begin to use what was stored in his big barns. Planning for retirement— preparing for life *before* death—is wise, but neglecting life *after* death is disastrous. If you accumulate wealth only to enrich yourself, with no concern for helping others, you will enter eternity empty-handed.

"There was a certain rich man who was splendidly clothed and who lived each day in luxury. At his door lay a diseased beggar named Lazarus. As Lazarus lay there longing for scraps from the rich man's table, the dogs would come and lick his open sores. Finally, the beggar died and was carried by the angels to be with Abraham. The rich man also died and was buried, and his soul went to the place of the dead. There, in torment, he saw Lazarus in the far distance with Abraham.

"The rich man shouted, 'Father Abraham, have some pity! Send Lazarus over here to dip the tip of his finger in water and cool my tongue, because I am in anguish in these flames.'

"But Abraham said to him, 'Son, remember that during your lifetime you had everything you wanted, and Lazarus had nothing. So now he is here being comforted, and you are in anguish. And besides, there is a great chasm separating us. Anyone who wanted to cross over to you from here is stopped at its edge, and no one there can cross over to us.'

"Then the rich man said, 'Please, Father Abraham, send him to my father's home. For I have five brothers, and I want him to warn them about this place of torment so they won't have to come here when they die.'

"But Abraham said, 'Moses and the prophets have warned them. Your brothers can read their writings anytime they want to.'

"The rich man replied, 'No, Father Abraham! But if someone is sent to them from the dead, then they will turn from their sins.'

"But Abraham said, 'If they won't listen to Moses and the prophets, they won't listen even if someone rises from the dead.'"
Luke 16:19-31

The Pharisees considered wealth to be proof of a person's righteousness. Jesus startled them with this story in which a diseased beggar is rewarded and a rich man is punished. The rich man did not go to hell because of his wealth but because he was selfish, refusing to feed Lazarus, take him in, or care for him. The rich man was hard-hearted in spite of his great blessings. The amount of money we have is not as important as the way we use it. What is your attitude toward your money and possessions? Do you hoard them selfishly, or do you use them to help others?

OVERCOMING TEMPTATION

"How terrible it will be for anyone who causes others to sin. Temptation to do wrong is inevitable, but how terrible it will be for the person who does the tempting. So if your hand or foot causes you to sin, cut it off and throw it away. It is better to enter heaven crippled or lame than to be thrown into the unquenchable fire with both of your hands and feet. And if your eye causes you to sin, gouge it out and throw it away. It is better to enter heaven half blind than to have two eyes and be thrown into hell." *Matthew 18:7-9*

We must remove stumbling blocks that cause us to sin. However, this does not mean to cut off a part of the body. For the church it means that any person, program, or teaching that threatens the spiritual growth of the body must be removed. For the individual, any relationship, practice, or activity that leads to sin should be stopped. Jesus says it would be better to go to heaven with one hand than to go to hell with both. Sin, of course, affects more than our hands; it affects our mind and heart.

"There will always be temptations to sin, but how terrible it will be for the person who does the tempting. It would be better to be thrown into the sea with a large millstone tied around the neck than to face the punishment in store for harming one of these little ones. I am warning you! If another believer sins, rebuke him; then if he repents, forgive him." *Luke 17:1-3*

Jesus may have been directing this warning at the religious leaders who taught their converts their own hypocritical ways. They were perpetuating an evil system. A person who teaches others has a solemn responsibility. Like a physician, a teacher should keep this ancient oath in mind: "First, do no harm."

"Keep alert and pray. Otherwise temptation will overpower you. For though the spirit is willing enough, the body is weak!"
Matthew 26:41

The way to overcome temptation is to keep alert and pray. Keeping alert means being aware of temptation, being sensitive to the strategies of the Devil, and being equipped to stand firm against them. Because temptation strikes where we are most vulnerable, we can't resist it alone. Prayer is essential because God's strength can shore up our defenses and defeat Satan's power.

"Pray that you will not be overcome by temptation." *Luke 22:40*

Jesus asked the disciples to pray that they would not fall into temptation because he knew that he would soon be leaving them. Jesus also knew that they would need extra strength to face the temptations ahead— temptations to run away or to deny their relationship with him. They were about to see Jesus die. Would they still think he was the Messiah? The disciples' strongest tempta- tion would undoubtedly be to think they had been deceived.

RESTORING
RELATIONSHIPS

"So if you are standing before the altar in
the Temple, offering a sacrifice to God, and
you suddenly remember that someone has
something against you, leave your sacrifice
there beside the altar. Go and be reconciled
to that person. Then come and offer your
sacrifice to God. Come to terms quickly
with your enemy before it is too late and
you are dragged into court, handed over to
an officer, and thrown in jail. I assure you
that you won't be free again until you have
paid the last penny." *Matthew 5:23-26*

Broken relationships can hinder our relationship with God. If we have a problem or grievance with someone, we should resolve the problem as soon as possible. We are hypocrites if we claim to love God while we hate others. Our attitudes toward others reflect our relationship with God.

"Stop judging others, and you will not be judged. For others will treat you as you treat them. Whatever measure you use in judging others, it will be used to measure how you are judged. And why worry about a speck in your friend's eye when you have a log in your own? How can you think of saying, 'Friend, let me help you get rid of that speck in your eye,' when you can't see past the log in your own eye? Hypocrite! First get rid of the log from your own eye; then perhaps you will see well enough to deal with the speck in your friend's eye." *Matthew 7:1-5*

Jesus' statement, "Stop judging," relates to the kind of hypocritical, judgmental attitude

that tears others down in order to build
oneself up. It is not a blanket statement to
overlook wrong behavior of others but
a call to be *discerning* rather than negative.
Jesus said to expose false prophets, and Paul
taught that we should exercise church discipline and trust God to be the final judge.

"If another believer sins against you, go pri-
vately and point out the fault. If the other person listens and confesses it, you have won
that person back. But if you are unsuccessful,
take one or two others with you and go back
again, so that everything you say may be con-
firmed by two or three witnesses. If that person still refuses to listen, take your case to the
church. If the church decides you are right,
but the other person won't accept it, treat that
person as a pagan or a corrupt tax collector."
Matthew 18:15-17

When someone wrongs us, we often do
the opposite of what Jesus recommends.
We turn away in hatred or resentment, seek
revenge, or engage in gossip. By contrast, we

should go to that person first, as difficult as
that may be. This is the model of reconcil-
iation Jesus set up for us.

**"I am warning you! If another believer sins,
rebuke him; then if he repeats, forgive him.
Even if he wrongs you seven times a day
and each time turns again and asks forgiveness, forgive him."** *Luke 17:3-4*

To rebuke does not mean to point out
every sin we see; it means to bring sin to
a person's attention with the purpose of
restoring him or her to God and to fellow
humans. When you feel that you must
rebuke another Christian for a sin, check
your attitudes before you speak. Do you
love that person? Are you willing to forgive?
Unless rebuke is tied to forgiveness, it will
not help the sinning person.

SATAN AND EVIL SPIRITS

"Any kingdom at war with itself is doomed. A city or home divided against itself is doomed. And if Satan is casting out Satan, he is fighting against himself. His own kingdom will not survive. And if I am empowered by the prince of demons, what about your own followers? They cast out demons, too, so they will judge you for what you have said. But if I am casting out demons by the Spirit of God, then the Kingdom of God has arrived among you. Let me illustrate this. You can't enter a strong man's house and rob him without first tying him

up. Only then can his house be robbed!"
Matthew 12:25-29

> At Jesus' birth, Satan's power and control
> were disrupted. In the wilderness Jesus
> overcame Satan's temptations, and at the
> Resurrection he defeated Satan's ultimate
> weapon—death. Eventually Satan will be
> constrained forever, and evil will no longer
> pervade the earth. Jesus has complete
> power and authority over Satan and all his
> forces.

"When an evil spirit leaves a person, it goes
into the desert, seeking rest but finding none.
Then it says, 'I will return to the person I
came from.' So it returns and finds its former
home empty, swept, and clean. Then the
spirit finds seven other spirits more evil than
itself, and they all enter the person and live
there. And so that person is worse off than
before. That will be the experience of this evil
generation." *Matthew 12:43-45*

> Jesus was describing the attitude of the
> nation of Israel and the religious leaders in

particular. Just cleaning up one's life without
filling it with God leaves plenty of room for
Satan to reenter. The book of Ezra records
how the people had rid themselves of idola-
try but failed to replace it with love for God
and obedience to him. Ridding our life of sin
is the first step. We must also take the second step: filling our life with God's Word and
the Holy Spirit. Unfilled and complacent
people are easy targets for Satan.

**"I saw Satan falling from heaven as a flash
of lightning! And I have given you authority over all the power of the enemy, and you
can walk among snakes and scorpions and
crush them. Nothing will injure you. But
don't rejoice just because evil spirits obey
you; rejoice because your names are registered as citizens of heaven."** *Luke 10:18-20*

Jesus may have been looking ahead to
his victory over Satan at the Cross. John
12:31-32 indicates that Satan would be
judged and driven out at the time of Jesus'
death. On the other hand, Jesus may have

been warning his disciples against pride. Perhaps he was referring to Isaiah 14:12-17, which begins, "How you are fallen from heaven, O shining star, son of the morning!" Some interpreters identify this verse with Satan and explain that Satan's pride led to all the evil we see on earth today. To Jesus' disciples, who were thrilled with their power over evil spirits ("snakes and scorpions"), he may have been giving this stern warning: "Yours is the kind of pride that led to Satan's downfall. Be careful!"

THE POWER OF FAITH

"I tell you the truth, I haven't seen faith like this in all the land of Israel! And I tell you this, that many Gentiles will come from all over the world and sit down with Abraham, Isaac, and Jacob at the feast in the Kingdom of Heaven. But many Israelites—those for whom the Kingdom was prepared—will be cast into outer darkness, where there will be weeping and gnashing of teeth. . . .

"Go on home. What you have believed has happened." *Matthew 8:10-13*

> Jesus told the crowd that many religious
> Jews who should be in the Kingdom would

be excluded because of their lack of faith.
Entrenched in their religious traditions, they
could not accept Christ and his new message. We must be careful not to become so
set in our religious habits that we expect
God to work only in specified ways. Don't
limit God by your mind-set and lack of faith.

"Daughter, be encouraged! Your faith has
made you well." *Matthew 9:22*

In our times of desperation, we don't have
to worry about the correct way to reach
out to God. We can simply reach out in
faith. He will respond.

"If you had faith as small as a mustard seed
you could say to this mountain, 'Move from
here to there,' and it would move. Nothing
would be impossible." *Matthew 17:20*

If you are facing a problem that seems as big
and immovable as a mountain, turn your eyes
from the mountain and look to Christ for
faith. Only then will you be able to overcome
the obstacles that may seem insurmountable.

"Anything is possible if a person believes."
Mark 9:23

> Jesus' words do not mean that we can auto-
> matically obtain anything we want if we just
> think positively. Jesus meant that anything is
> possible if we believe, because nothing is
> too difficult for God. We cannot have every-
> thing we pray for as if by magic, but with
> faith, we can have everything we need
> to serve him.

"Your faith has saved you; go in peace."
Luke 7:50

> The Pharisees believed that only God could
> forgive sins. When Jesus said this to the adul-
> terous woman, they wondered why this
> man Jesus was saying that her sins were for-
> given. They did not grasp the fact that Jesus
> was indeed God.

**"Even if you had faith as small as a mustard
seed . . . you could say to this mulberry tree,
'May God uproot you and throw you into
the sea,' and it would obey you!"** *Luke 17:6*

211

A mustard seed is small, but it is alive and growing. Almost invisible at first, it will begin to spread, first under the ground, and then it will become visible. Like a tiny seed, a small amount of genuine faith in God will take root and grow. Although each change will be gradual and possibly imperceptible, soon this faith will have produced major results that will uproot and destroy competing loyalties. We don't need more faith; a tiny seed of faith is enough if it is alive and growing.

THE WAY OF HUMILITY

"If you are invited to a wedding feast, don't always head for the best seat. What if someone more respected than you has also been invited? The host will say, 'Let this person sit here instead.' Then you will be embarrassed and will have to take whatever seat is left at the foot of the table!

"Do this instead—sit at the foot of the table. Then when your host sees you, he will come and say, 'Friend, we have a better place than this for you!' Then you will be honored in front of all the other guests. For the proud will be humbled, but the humble will be honored." *Luke 14:8-11*

> How can we humble ourselves? Some people try to give the appearance of humility in order to manipulate others. Others think that humility means putting themselves down. Truly humble people compare themselves only to Christ, realize their sinfulness, and understand their limitations. On the other hand, they also recognize their gifts and strengths and are willing to use them as Christ directs. Humility is not self-degradation; it is realistic self-assessment and commitment to serve.

"The greatest among you must be a servant. But those who exalt themselves will be humbled, and those who humble them- selves will be exalted." *Matthew 23:11-12*

> Jesus challenged society's norms. To him, great- ness comes from serving—giving of yourself to help God and others. Service keeps us aware of others' needs, and it stops us from focusing only on ourselves. Jesus came as a servant. What kind of greatness do you seek?

"If you try to keep your life for yourself, you
will lose it. But if you give up your life for me,
you will find true life. And how do you benefit if you gain the whole world but lose your
own soul in the process? Is anything worth
more than your soul?" *Matthew 16:25-26*

> Real discipleship implies real commitment—
> pledging our whole existence to his service.
> If we try to save our physical life from death,
> pain, or discomfort, we may risk losing eter-
> nal life. If we protect ourselves from the pain
> God calls us to suffer, we begin to die spiritu-
> ally and emotionally. Our life turns inward,
> and we lose our intended purpose. When
> we give our life in service to Christ, however,
> we discover the real purpose of living.

True Happiness

"God blesses those who realize their need for him, for the Kingdom of Heaven is given to them. God blesses those who mourn, for they will be comforted. God blesses those who are gentle and lowly, for the whole earth will belong to them. God blesses those who are hungry and thirsty for justice, for they will receive it in full. God blesses those who are merciful, for they will be shown mercy. God blesses those whose hearts are pure, for they will see God. God blesses those who work for peace, for they will be called the children of

God. God blesses those who are persecuted because they live for God, for the Kingdom of Heaven is theirs.

"God blesses you when you are mocked and persecuted and lied about because you are my followers. Be happy about it! Be very glad! For a great reward awaits you in heaven. And remember, the ancient prophets were persecuted, too." *Matthew 5:3-12*

> Each beatitude tells how to be *blessed* by God. *Blessed* means more than happiness. It implies the fortunate or enviable state of those who are in God's Kingdom. The Beatitudes don't promise laughter, pleasure, or earthly prosperity. Being "blessed" by God means experiencing hope and joy, independent of outward circumstances. To find hope and joy, the deepest forms of happiness, follow Jesus no matter what the cost.

"God blesses you who are poor, for the Kingdom of God is given to you. God blesses you who are hungry now, for you will be satisfied. God blesses you who weep now, for the time will come when you will laugh with joy. God blesses you who are hated and excluded and mocked and cursed because you are identified with me, the Son of Man.

"When that happens, rejoice! Yes, leap for joy! For a great reward awaits you in heaven. And remember, the ancient prophets were also treated that way by your ancestors."
Luke 6:20-23

> These Beatitudes describe what it means to be Christ's follower. They contrast Kingdom values with worldly values, showing what Christ's followers can expect from the world and what God will give them. They contrast fake piety with true humility, and finally they show how Old Testament expectations are fulfilled in God's Kingdom.

"You believe because you have seen me. Blessed are those who haven't seen me and believe anyway." *John 20:29*

> Some people think they would believe in Jesus if they could see a definite sign or miracle. But Jesus says we are blessed if we

can believe without seeing. We have all the
proof we need in the words of the Bible
and the testimony of believers. A physical
appearance would not make Jesus any more
real to us than he is now.

TRUE RICHES

"If you give even a cup of cold water to one of the least of my followers, you will surely be rewarded." *Matthew 10:42*

How much we love God can be measured by how well we treat others. Jesus' example of giving a cup of cold water to someone who thirsts is a good model of unselfish service. God notices every good deed we do or don't do as if he were the one receiving it. Is there something unselfish you can do for someone else today? Although no one else may see you, God will notice.

"If you want to be perfect, go and sell all you have and give the money to the poor, and you will have treasure in heaven. Then come, follow me." *Matthew 19:21*

> Should all believers sell everything they own? No. We are responsible to care for our own needs and the needs of our families so we don't burden others. We should, however, be willing to give up anything if God asks us to do so. This kind of attitude allows nothing to come between us and God and keeps us from using our God-given possessions selfishly. If you are comforted by the fact that Christ did not tell all his followers to sell all their possessions, then you may be too attached to what you have.

"Why berate her for doing such a good thing to me? You will always have the poor among you, but I will not be here with you much longer. She has poured this perfume on me to prepare my body for burial. I assure you, wherever the Good News is preached throughout the world, this woman's deed will be talked about in her memory." *Matthew 26:10-13*

> Here Jesus brought back to mind Deuteronomy 15:11: "There will always be some among you who are poor." This statement does not justify ignoring the needs of the poor. Scripture continually exhorts us to care for the needy. The passage in Deuteronomy continues: "That is why I am commanding you to share your resources freely with the poor and with other Israelites in need." By saying this, Jesus highlighted the special sacrifice Mary had made for him.

"He will give you all you need from day to day if you make the Kingdom of God your primary concern.

"So don't be afraid, little flock. For it gives your Father great happiness to give you the Kingdom.

"Sell what you have and give to those in need. This will store up treasure for you in heaven! And the purses of heaven have no holes in them. Your treasure will be safe—no thief can steal it and no moth can destroy it. Wherever your treasure is, there your heart and thoughts will also be." *Luke 12:31-34*

> Money seen as an end in itself quickly traps us and cuts us off from both God and the needy. The key to using money wisely is to see how much we can use for God's purposes, not how much we can accumulate for ourselves. Does God's love touch your wallet? Does your money free you to help others? If so, you are storing up lasting treasures in heaven. If your financial goals and possessions hinder you from giving generously, loving others, or serving God, sell what you must to bring your life into perspective.

"I assure you . . . this poor widow has given more than all the rest of them. For they have given a tiny part of their surplus, but she, poor as she is, has given everything she has." *Luke 21:3-4*

> In contrast to the way most of us handle our money, this widow gave all she had

to live on. When we consider ourselves generous in giving a small percentage of our income to the Lord, we resemble those who gave "a tiny part of their surplus." Jesus admired the widow's generous and sacrificial giving. As believers, we should consider increasing our giving—whether money, time, or talents—to a point beyond mere convenience.

TRUE RIGHTEOUSNESS

"But I warn you—unless you obey God better than the teachers of religious law and the Pharisees do, you can't enter the Kingdom of Heaven at all!" *Matthew 5:20*

The Pharisees were exacting and scrupulous in their attempts to follow their laws. So how could Jesus reasonably call us to greater obedience than theirs? The Pharisees' weakness was that they were content to obey the laws outwardly without allowing God to change their hearts (or attitudes). Jesus was saying, therefore, that the *quality* of our goodness should be greater than that of the Pharisees. They looked pious, but they were far from the Kingdom of Heaven. God judges our heart as well as our deeds, for it is in the heart that our real allegiance lies. Be just as concerned about your attitudes that people don't see as about your actions that are seen by all.

"Take care! Don't do your good deeds publicly, to be admired, because then you will lose the reward from your Father in heaven. When you give a gift to someone in need, don't shout about it as the hypocrites do— blowing trumpets in the synagogues and streets to call attention to their acts of charity! I assure you, they have received all the reward they will ever get. But when you give to someone, don't tell your left hand what your right hand is doing. Give your gifts in secret, and your Father, who knows all secrets, will reward you." *Matthew 6:1-4*

The term *hypocrites*, as used here, describes people who do good acts for appearance only—not out of compassion or other good motives. Their actions may be good, but their motives are hollow. The attention they may get is their only reward, but God will reward those who are sincere in their faith and acts of charity.

"A tree is identified by its fruit. Make a tree good, and its fruit will be good. Make a tree bad, and its fruit will be bad. You brood of snakes! How could evil men like you speak what is good and right? For whatever is in your heart determines what you say. A good person produces good words from a good heart, and an evil person produces evil words from an evil heart. And I tell you this, that you must give an account on judgment day of every idle word you speak. The words you say now reflect your fate then; either you will be justified by them or you will be condemned." *Matthew 12:33-37*

Jesus reminds us that what we say reveals what is in our heart. What kinds of words come from your mouth? That is an indication of what is in your heart. You can't solve your heart problem, however, just by cleaning up your speech. You must allow the Holy Spirit to fill you with new attitudes and motives, so your speech will be cleansed at its source.

"It is the thought-life that defiles you. For from within, out of a person's heart, come evil thoughts, sexual immorality, theft, murder, adultery, greed, wickedness, deceit, eagerness for lustful pleasure, envy, slander, pride, and foolishness. All these vile things come from within; they are what defile you and make you unacceptable to God." *Mark 7:20-23*

An evil action begins with a single thought. Allowing our mind to dwell on lust, envy, hatred, or revenge will lead to sin. Don't defile yourself by focusing on evil. Instead, follow Paul's advice in Philippians 4:8 and think about what is true, honorable, right, pure, lovely, and admirable.

"No one lights a lamp and then hides it or puts it under a basket. Instead, it is put on

a lampstand to give light to all who enter the room. Your eye is a lamp for your body. A pure eye lets sunshine into your soul. But an evil eye shuts out the light and plunges you into darkness. Make sure that the light you think you have is not really darkness. If you are filled with light, with no dark corners, then your whole life will be radiant, as though a floodlight is shining on you."
Luke 11:33-36

The lamp is Christ; the eye represents spiritual understanding and insight. Evil desires make the eye less sensitive and blot out the light of Christ's presence. If you have a hard time seeing God at work in the world and in your life, check your vision. Are any sinful desires blinding you to Christ?

TRUE WORSHIP

"Believe me, the time is coming when it will no longer matter whether you worship the Father here or in Jerusalem. You Samaritans know so little about the one you worship, while we Jews know all about him, for salvation comes through the Jews. But the time is coming and is already here when true worshipers will worship the Father in spirit and in truth. The Father is looking for anyone who will worship him that way. For God is Spirit, so those who worship him must worship in spirit and in truth." *John 4:21-24*

"God is Spirit" means that he is not a physical being limited to one place. He is present everywhere, and he can be worshiped anywhere, at any time. It is not *where* we worship that counts but *how* we worship. Is your worship genuine and true? Do you have the Holy Spirit's help? How does the Holy Spirit help us worship? The Holy Spirit prays for us, teaches us the words of Christ, and tells us we are loved.

Warnings
of Jesus

WARNINGS ABOUT
FALSE TEACHERS

"Beware of false prophets who come disguised as harmless sheep, but are really wolves that will tear you apart. You can detect them by the way they act, just as you can identify a tree by its fruit. You don't pick grapes from thornbushes, or figs from thistles. A healthy tree produces good fruit, and an unhealthy tree produces bad fruit. A good tree can't produce bad fruit, and a bad tree can't produce good fruit. So every tree that does not produce good fruit is chopped down and thrown into the fire. Yes, the way to identify a tree or a person is by the kind of fruit that is produced.

"Not all people who sound religious are really godly. They may refer to me as 'Lord,' but they still won't enter the Kingdom of Heaven. The decisive issue is whether they obey my Father in heaven." *Matthew 7:15-21*

> There were false prophets in Jesus' day, and we have them today. They are the popular leaders who tell people what they want to hear, such as "God wants you to be rich," "Do whatever you desire," or "There is no such thing as sin or hell." Jesus said false teachers would come, and he warned his disciples, as he warns us, not to listen to their dangerous words.

"Don't let anyone mislead you. For many will come in my name, saying, 'I am the Messiah.' They will lead many astray. And wars will break out near and far, but don't panic. Yes, these things must come, but the end won't follow immediately. The nations and kingdoms will proclaim war against each other, and there will be famines and earthquakes in many parts of the world. But all this will be only the beginning of the horrors to come.

"Then you will be arrested, persecuted, and killed. You will be hated all over the world because of your allegiance to me. And many will turn away from me and betray and hate each other. And many false prophets will appear and will lead many people astray. Sin will be rampant everywhere, and the love of many will grow cold. But those who endure to the end will be saved." *Matthew 24:4-13*

> The disciples asked Jesus for a sign of his coming and the end of the age. Jesus' first response was "Don't let anyone mislead you." The fact is that whenever we look for signs, we become very susceptible to being deceived. There are many "false prophets" around today with counterfeit signs of spiritual power and authority. The only sure way to keep from being deceived is to focus on Christ and his words. Don't look for special signs, and don't spend time looking at other people. Look at Christ.

WARNINGS
ABOUT HYPOCRISY

"And when you fast, don't make it obvious, as the hypocrites do, who try to look pale and disheveled so people will admire them for their fasting. I assure you, that is the only reward they will ever get. But when you fast, comb your hair and wash your face. Then no one will suspect you are fasting, except your Father, who knows what you do in secret. And your Father, who knows all secrets, will reward you." *Matthew 6:16-18*

In these verses, Jesus is not condemning fasting, but hypocrisy—fasting in order to gain public approval. Many Pharisees voluntarily fasted twice a week to impress the people with their "holiness." Jesus commended acts of self-sacrifice done quietly and sincerely. He wanted people to adopt spiritual disciplines for the right reasons, not from a selfish desire for praise.

"The teachers of religious law and the Pharisees are the official interpreters of the Scriptures. So practice and obey whatever they say to you, but don't follow their example. For they don't practice what they teach. They crush you with impossible religious demands and never lift a finger to help ease the burden."
Matthew 23:2-4

The Pharisees' traditions and their interpretations and applications of the laws had become as important to them as God's law itself. Their laws were not all bad— some were beneficial. Problems arose when the religious leaders (1) held that man-made rules were equal to God's laws,

(2) told the people to obey these rules but did not do so themselves, or (3) obeyed the rules, not to honor God but to make themselves look good. Usually Jesus did not condemn what the Pharisees taught but what they *were*—hypocrites.

"How terrible it will be for you teachers of religious law and you Pharisees. Hypocrites! For you won't let others enter the Kingdom of Heaven, and you won't go in yourselves. How terrible it will be for you teachers of religious law and you Pharisees. Hypocrites! You shamelessly cheat widows out of their property, and then, to cover up the kind of people you really are, you make long prayers in public. Because of this, your punishment will be the greater." *Matthew 23:13-14 [Some early manuscripts do not include verse 14.]*

Being a religious leader in Jerusalem was very different from being a pastor in a secular society today. Israel's history, culture, and daily life centered around its relationship with God. The religious leaders were the best known, most powerful, and most respected of all leaders. Jesus made these stinging accusations because the leaders' hunger for more power, money, and status had made them lose sight of God, and their blindness was spreading to the whole nation.

"Beware of these teachers of religious law! For they love to parade in flowing robes and to have everyone bow to them as they walk in the marketplaces. And how they love the seats of honor in the synagogues and at banquets." *Mark 12:38-39*

Jesus warned against trying to make a good impression. These teachers of religious law were religious hypocrites who had no love for God. True followers of Christ are not distinguished by showy spirituality. Reading the Bible, praying in public, or following church rituals can be phony if the motive for doing them is to be noticed or honored. Let your actions be consistent with your beliefs. Live for Christ, even when no one is looking.

"How terrible it will be for you teachers of religious law and you Pharisees. Hypocrites! For you are careful to tithe even the tiniest part of your income, but you ignore the important things of the law—justice, mercy, and faith. You should tithe, yes, but you should not leave undone the more important things. Blind guides! You strain your water so you won't accidentally swallow a gnat; then you swallow a camel!"
Matthew 23:23-24

> It's possible to obey the details of the law but still be disobedient in our general behavior. For example, we could be very precise and faithful about giving 10 percent of our money to God but refuse to give one minute of our time helping others. Tithing is important, but giving a tithe does not exempt us from fulfilling God's other directives.

"How terrible it will be for you teachers of religious law and you Pharisees. Hypocrites! You are like whitewashed tombs—beautiful on the outside but filled on the inside with

dead people's bones and all sorts of impurity.
You try to look like upright people outwardly,
but inside your hearts are filled with hypocrisy and lawlessness." *Matthew 23:27-28*

> Jesus condemned the Pharisees and religious
> leaders for outwardly appearing upright and
> holy but inwardly remaining full of corrup-
> tion and greed. Living our Christianity merely
> as a show for others is like washing only the
> outside of a cup. When we are clean on the
> inside, our cleanliness on the outside won't
> be a sham.

WARNINGS OF PERSECUTION

"Look, I am sending you out as sheep among wolves. Be as wary as snakes and harmless as doves. But beware! For you will be handed over to the courts and beaten in the synagogues. And you must stand trial before governors and kings because you are my followers. This will be your opportunity to tell them about me—yes, to witness to the world. When you are arrested, don't worry about what to say in your defense, because you will be given the right words at the right time. For it won't be you doing the talking—it will be the Spirit of your Father speaking through you.

"Brother will betray brother to death, fathers will betray their own children, and children will rise against their parents and cause them to be killed. And everyone will hate you because of your allegiance to me. But those who endure to the end will be saved. When you are persecuted in one town, flee to the next. I assure you that I, the Son of Man, will return before you have reached all the towns of Israel." *Matthew 10:16-23*

> Enduring to the end is not a way to be saved but the evidence that a person is really committed to Jesus. Persistence is not a means to earn salvation; it is the by-product of a truly devoted life.

"I command you to love each other. When the world hates you, remember it hated me before it hated you. The world would love you if you belonged to it, but you don't. I chose you to come out of the world, and so it hates you. Do you remember what I told you? 'A servant is not greater than the master.' Since they persecuted me, naturally they will

persecute you. And if they had listened to me,
they would listen to you! The people of the
world will hate you because you belong to
me, for they don't know God who sent me."
John 15:17-21

> Christians will get plenty of hatred from the
> world; from each other we need love and
> support. Do you allow small problems to get
> in the way of loving other believers? Jesus
> commands that you love them, and he will
> give you the strength to do it.

"But the time is coming—in fact, it is
already here—when you will be scattered,
each one going his own way, leaving me
alone. Yet I am not alone because the
Father is with me. I have told you all this
so that you may have peace in me. Here
on earth you will have many trials and
sorrows. But take heart, because I have
overcome the world." *John 16:32-33*

> In these verses, Jesus told his disciples to
> take courage. In spite of the inevitable
> struggles they would face, they would not

be alone. Jesus does not abandon us to
our struggles either. If we remember that
the ultimate victory has already been won,
we can claim the peace of Christ in our
most troublesome times.

WARNINGS OF COMING JUDGMENT

"On judgment day many will tell me, 'Lord, Lord, we prophesied in your name and cast out demons in your name and performed many miracles in your name.' But I will reply, 'I never knew you. Go away; the things you did were unauthorized.'" *Matthew 7:22-23*

> Judgment day is the final day of reckoning when God will settle all accounts, judging sin and rewarding faith.

"The Kingdom of Heaven is like a farmer who planted good seed in his field. But that night as everyone slept, his enemy came and planted weeds among the wheat. When the crop began to grow and produce grain, the weeds also grew. The farmer's servants came and told him, 'Sir, the field where you planted that good seed is full of weeds!'

"'An enemy has done it!' the farmer exclaimed.

"'Shall we pull out the weeds?' they asked.

"He replied, 'No, you'll hurt the wheat if you do. Let both grow together until the harvest. Then I will tell the harvesters to sort out the weeds and burn them and to put the wheat in the barn.'" *Matthew 13:24-30*

The young weeds and the young blades of wheat look the same and can't be distinguished until they are grown and ready for harvest. Weeds (unbelievers) and wheat (believers) must live side by side in this world. God allows unbelievers to remain for a while, just as a farmer allows weeds to remain in his field so the surrounding wheat isn't uprooted with them. At the harvest, however, the weeds will be uprooted and

thrown into the fire. God's harvest (judgment) of all people is coming. We are to
make ourselves ready by making sure that
our faith is sincere.

"The Kingdom of Heaven is like a fishing net
that is thrown into the water and gathers fish
of every kind. When the net is full, they drag
it up onto the shore, sit down, sort the good
fish into crates, and throw the bad ones away.
That is the way it will be at the end of the
world. The angels will come and separate the
wicked people from the godly, throwing the
wicked into the fire. There will be weeping
and gnashing of teeth. Do you understand?"
Matthew 13:47-51

The parable of the fishing net has the same
meaning as the parable of the wheat and
weeds. We are to obey God and tell others
about his grace and goodness, but we cannot dictate who is and who is not part of
the Kingdom of Heaven. This sorting will be
done at the last judgment by those infinitely
more qualified than we are.

"But when the Son of Man comes in his glory, and all the angels with him, then he will sit upon his glorious throne. All the nations will be gathered in his presence, and he will separate them as a shepherd separates the sheep from the goats. He will place the sheep at his right hand and the goats at his left. Then the King will say to those on the right, 'Come, you who are blessed by my Father, inherit the Kingdom prepared for you from the foundation of the world. For I was hungry, and you fed me. I was thirsty, and you gave me a drink. I was a stranger, and you invited me into your home. I was naked, and you gave me clothing. I was sick, and you cared for me. I was in prison, and you visited me.'

"Then these righteous ones will reply, 'Lord, when did we ever see you hungry and feed you? Or thirsty and give you something to drink? Or a stranger and show you hospitality? Or naked and give you clothing? When did we ever see you sick or in prison, and visit you?' And the King will tell them, 'I assure you, when you did it to one of the least of these my brothers and sisters, you were doing it to me!'

"Then the King will turn to those on the left and say, 'Away with you, you cursed ones, into the eternal fire prepared for the Devil and his demons! For I was hungry, and you didn't feed me. I was thirsty, and you didn't give me anything to drink. I was a stranger, and you didn't invite me into your home. I was naked, and you gave me no clothing. I was sick and in prison, and you didn't visit me.'

"Then they will reply, 'Lord, when did we ever see you hungry or thirsty or a stranger or naked or sick or in prison, and not help you?' And he will answer, 'I assure you, when you refused to help the least of these my brothers and sisters, you were refusing to help me.' And they will go away into eternal punishment, but the righteous will go into eternal life." *Matthew 25:31-46*

God will separate his obedient followers from pretenders and unbelievers. The real evidence of our belief is the way we act. To treat all persons we encounter as if they were Jesus is no easy task. What we do for others demonstrates what we really think about Jesus' words to us: Feed the hungry, give the homeless a place to stay, look after the sick. How well do your actions separate you from pretenders and unbelievers?

SIGNS OF THE END TIMES

"Don't let anyone mislead you, because
many will come in my name, claiming to
be the Messiah. They will lead many astray.
And wars will break out near and far, but
don't panic. Yes, these things must come,
but the end won't follow immediately.
Nations and kingdoms will proclaim war
against each other, and there will be earthquakes in many parts of the world, and famines. But all this will be only the beginning
of the horrors to come. But when these
things begin to happen, watch out! You will
be handed over to the courts and beaten in

the synagogues. You will be accused before governors and kings of being my followers. This will be your opportunity to tell them about me. And the Good News must first be preached to every nation. But when you are arrested and stand trial, don't worry about what to say in your defense. Just say what God tells you to. Then it is not you who will be speaking, but the Holy Spirit."
Mark 13:5-11

What are the signs of the end times? There have been people in every generation since Christ's resurrection claiming to know exactly when Jesus would return. No one has been right yet, however, because Christ will return on God's timetable, not ours. Jesus predicted that before his return, many believers would be misled by false teachers claiming to have revelations from God.

According to Scripture, another clear sign of Christ's return will be his unmistakable appearance in the clouds, which will be seen by all people. In other words, you do not have to wonder whether a certain person is the Messiah or whether these are the "end times." When Jesus returns *you will know* beyond a doubt, because it will be evident to all true believers. Beware of groups who claim special knowledge of Christ's return because no one knows when that time will be. Be cautious about saying, "This is it!" but be bold in your total commitment to have your heart and life ready for Christ's return.

"Brother will betray brother to death, fathers will betray their own children, and children will rise against their parents and cause them to be killed. And everyone will hate you because of your allegiance to me. But those who endure to the end will be saved." *Mark 13:12-13*

To believe in Jesus and "endure to the end" will take perseverance because our faith will be challenged and opposed. Severe trials will sift true Christians from fair-weather believers. Enduring to the end does not earn salvation for us but marks

259

us as already saved. The assurance of our salvation will keep us strong in times of persecution.

"The time will come when you will see the sacrilegious object that causes desecration standing where it should not be"—reader, pay attention! "Then those in Judea must flee to the hills. A person outside the house must not go back into the house to pack. A person in the field must not return even to get a coat. How terrible it will be for pregnant women and for mothers nursing their babies in those days. And pray that your flight will not be in winter. For those will be days of greater horror than at any time since God created the world. And it will never happen again. In fact, unless the Lord shortens that time of calamity, the entire human race will be destroyed. But for the sake of his chosen ones he has shortened those days.

"And then if anyone tells you, 'Look, here is the Messiah,' or, 'There he is,' don't pay any attention. For false messiahs and false prophets will rise up and perform miraculous signs and wonders so as to deceive, if possible, even God's chosen ones. Watch out! I have warned you!

"At that time, after those horrible days end,

> the sun will be darkened,
> the moon will not give light,
> the stars will fall from the sky,
> and the powers of heaven will be shaken.

Then everyone will see the Son of Man arrive on the clouds with great power and glory. And he will send forth his angels to gather together his chosen ones from all over the world—from the farthest ends of the earth and heaven.

"Now, learn a lesson from the fig tree. When its buds become tender and its leaves begin to sprout, you know without being told that summer is near. Just so, when you see the events I've described

beginning to happen, you can be sure that his return is very near, right at the door. I assure you, this generation will not pass from the scene until all these events have taken place. Heaven and earth will disappear, but my words will remain forever."
Mark 13:14-31

> In Jesus' day the world seemed concrete, dependable, and permanent. In our day many people fear its destruction by nuclear war. Jesus tells us, however, that even if the earth passes away, the truth of his words will never be changed or abolished. God and his Word provide the only stability in our unstable world. How shortsighted people are who spend all their time and energy learning about this temporary world and accumulating its possessions, while neglecting the Bible and its eternal truths!

"No one knows the day or hour when these things will happen, not even the angels in heaven or the Son himself. Only the Father knows. And since you don't know when

they will happen, stay alert and keep watch."
Mark 13:32-33

When Jesus said that even he did not know
the time of the end, he was affirming his
humanity. Of course God the Father knows
the time, and Jesus and the Father are one.
But when Jesus became a man, he voluntarily gave up the unlimited use of his divine
attributes during his time on earth.

The emphasis of these verses is not on
Jesus' lack of knowledge but on the fact that
no one knows. It is known only to God the
Father to be revealed when he wills. No one
can predict through Scripture or science the
exact day of Jesus' return. Jesus teaches that
preparation, not calculation, is needed.

Other Illustrations Jesus Used

JESUS' RADICAL
MESSAGE

"No one tears a piece of cloth from a new
garment and uses it to patch an old garment. For then the new garment would be
torn, and the patch wouldn't even match
the old garment. And no one puts new
wine into old wineskins. The new wine
would burst the old skins, spilling the wine
and ruining the skins. New wine must be
put into new wineskins. But no one who
drinks the old wine seems to want the fresh
and the new. 'The old is better,' they say."
Luke 5:36-39

Wineskins were goatskins sewn together at the edges to form watertight bags. Because new wine expands as it ages, it had to be put into new, pliable wineskins. A used skin, having become more rigid, would burst and spill the wine. Like old wineskins, the Pharisees were too rigid to accept Jesus, who could not be contained in their traditions or rules. Christianity required new approaches, new traditions, new structures. Our church programs and ministries should not be so structured that there is no room for a fresh touch of the Spirit, a new method, or a new idea. We, too, must be careful that our heart does not become so rigid that it prevents us from accepting new ways of thinking that Christ brings. We need to keep our heart pliable so we can accept Jesus' life-changing message.

READY FOR THE KINGDOM

"The coming of the Son of Man can be compared with that of a man who left home to go on a trip. He gave each of his employees instructions about the work they were to do, and he told the gatekeeper to watch for his return. So keep a sharp lookout! For you do not know when the homeowner will return—at evening, midnight, early dawn, or late daybreak. Don't let him find you sleeping when he arrives without warning. What I say to you I say to everyone: Watch for his return!" *Mark 13:34-37*

How should we live while we wait for Christ's return? (1) We are not to be misled by confusing claims or speculative interpretations of what will happen. (2) We should not be afraid to tell people about Christ, despite what they might say or do to us. (3) We must stand firm by faith and not be surprised by persecution. (4) We must be morally alert, obedient to the commands for living found in God's Word. These words were not given to promote discussions on prophetic timetables but to stimulate right living for God in a world that largely ignores him.

"The Kingdom of Heaven can be illustrated by the story of ten bridesmaids who took their lamps and went to meet the bridegroom. Five of them were foolish, and five were wise. The five who were foolish took no oil for their lamps, but the other five were wise enough to take along extra oil. When the bridegroom was delayed, they all lay down and slept. At midnight they were roused by the shout, 'Look, the bridegroom is coming! Come out and welcome him!'

"All the bridesmaids got up and prepared their lamps. Then the five foolish ones asked the others, 'Please give us some of your oil because our lamps are going out.' But the others replied, 'We don't have enough for all of us. Go to a shop and buy some for yourselves.'

"But while they were gone to buy oil, the bridegroom came, and those who were ready went in with him to the marriage feast, and the door was locked. Later, when the other five bridesmaids returned, they stood outside, calling, 'Sir, open the door for us!' But he called back, 'I don't know you!'

"So stay awake and be prepared, because you do not know the day or hour of my return." *Matthew 25:1-13*

In this parable, Jesus clarifies what it means to be ready for his return and how to live until he comes. When Jesus returns to take his people to heaven, we must be ready. Spiritual preparation cannot be bought or borrowed at the last minute. Our relationship with God must be our own.

"The Kingdom of Heaven can be illustrated by the story of a king who prepared a great wedding feast for his son. Many guests were invited, and when the banquet was ready, he sent his servants to notify everyone that it was time to come. But they all refused! So he sent other servants to tell them, 'The feast has been prepared, and choice meats have been cooked. Everything is ready. Hurry!' But the guests he had invited ignored them and went about their business, one to his farm, another to his store. Others seized his messengers and treated them shamefully, even killing some of them.

"Then the king became furious. He sent out his army to destroy the murderers and burn their city. And he said to his servants, 'The wedding feast is ready, and the guests I invited aren't worthy of the honor. Now go out to the street corners and invite everyone you see.'

"So the servants brought in everyone they could find, good and bad alike, and the banquet hall was filled with guests. But when the king came in to meet the guests, he noticed a man who wasn't wearing the proper clothes for a wedding. 'Friend,' he asked, 'how is it that you are here without wedding clothes?' And the man had no reply. The king said to his aides, 'Bind him hand and foot and throw him out into the outer darkness, where there is weeping and gnashing of teeth.' For many are called, but few are chosen." *Matthew 22:2-14*

In Jesus' culture, two invitations were expected when banquets were given. The first asked the guests to attend; the second announced that all was ready. In this story the king invited his guests three times, and each time they rejected his invitation.

God wants us to join him at his banquet, which will last for eternity. That's why he sends us invitations again and again. Have you accepted his invitation?

THE LAST WILL BE FIRST

"For the Kingdom of Heaven is like the owner of an estate who went out early one morning to hire workers for his vineyard. He agreed to pay the normal daily wage and sent them out to work.

"At nine o'clock in the morning he was passing through the marketplace and saw some people standing around doing nothing. So he hired them, telling them he would pay them whatever was right at the end of the day. At noon and again around three o'clock he did the same thing. At five o'clock that evening he was in town again and saw some more people standing around. He asked them, 'Why haven't you been working today?'

"They replied, 'Because no one hired us.'

"The owner of the estate told them, 'Then go on out and join the others in my vineyard.'

"That evening he told the foreman to call the workers in and pay them, beginning with the last workers first. When those hired at five o'clock were paid, each received a full day's wage. When those hired earlier came to get their pay, they assumed they would receive more. But they, too, were paid a day's wage. When they received their pay, they protested, 'Those people worked only one hour, and yet you've paid them just as much as you paid us who worked all day in the scorching heat.'

"He answered one of them, 'Friend, I haven't been unfair! Didn't you agree to work all day for the usual wage? Take it and go. I wanted to pay this last worker the same as you. Is it against the law for

me to do what I want with my money?
Should you be angry because I am kind?'

"And so it is, that many who are first now
will be last then; and those who are last
now will be first then." *Matthew 20:1-16*

> Jesus further clarified the membership rules
> of the Kingdom of Heaven: Entrance is by
> God's grace alone. In this parable, God is the
> owner of the estate, and believers are the
> workers. This parable speaks especially to
> those who feel superior because of heritage
> or position, to those who feel superior
> because they have spent so much time with
> Christ, and to new believers as reassurance
> of God's grace.

THE REJECTION OF JESUS

"A man planted a vineyard, built a wall around it, dug a pit for pressing out the grape juice, and built a lookout tower. Then he leased the vineyard to tenant farmers and moved to another country. At grape-picking time he sent one of his servants to collect his share of the crop. But the farmers grabbed the servant, beat him up, and sent him back empty-handed.

"The owner then sent another servant, but they beat him over the head and treated him shamefully. The next servant he sent was killed. Others who were sent were either beaten or killed, until there was only one left—his son whom he loved dearly. The owner finally sent him, thinking, 'Surely they will respect my son.'

"But the farmers said to one another, 'Here comes the heir to this estate. Let's kill him and get the estate for ourselves!' So they grabbed him and murdered him and threw his body out of the vineyard.

"What do you suppose the owner of the vineyard will do? . . . I'll tell you—he will come and kill them all and lease the vineyard to others." *Mark 12:1-9*

In this parable, the man who planted the vineyard is God. The vineyard is the nation of Israel, and the tenant farmers are Israel's religious leaders. The servants are the prophets and priests who remained faithful to God, the son is Jesus, and the others are the Gentiles. By telling this story, Jesus exposed the religious leaders' plot to kill him and warned that their sins would be punished.

WISE STEWARDSHIP

"The Kingdom of Heaven can be illustrated by the story of a man going on a trip. He called together his servants and gave them money to invest for him while he was gone. He gave five bags of gold to one, two bags of gold to another, and one bag of gold to the last—dividing it in proportion to their abilities—and then left on his trip. The servant who received the five bags of gold began immediately to invest the money and soon doubled it. The servant with two bags of gold also went right to work and doubled it. But the servant who received the one bag of gold dug a hole in the ground and hid the master's money for safekeeping.

"After a long time their master returned from his trip and called them to give an account of how they had used his money. The servant to whom he had entrusted the five bags of gold said, 'Sir, you gave me five bags of gold to invest, and I have doubled the amount.' The master was full of praise. 'Well done, my good and faithful servant. You have been faithful in handling this small amount, so now I will give you many more responsibilities. Let's celebrate together!'

"Next came the servant who had received the two bags of gold, with the report, 'Sir, you gave me two bags of gold to invest, and I have doubled the amount.' The master said, 'Well done, my good and faithful servant. You have been faithful in handling this small amount, so now I will give you many more responsibilities. Let's celebrate together!'

"Then the servant with the one bag of gold came and said, 'Sir, I know you are a hard man, harvesting crops you didn't plant and gathering crops you didn't cultivate. I was afraid I would lose your money, so I hid it in the earth and here it is.'

"But the master replied, 'You wicked and lazy servant! You think I'm a hard man, do you, harvesting crops I didn't plant and gathering crops I didn't cultivate? Well, you should at least have put my money into the bank so I could have some interest. Take the money from this servant and give it to the one with the ten bags of gold. To those who use well what they are given, even more will be given, and they will have an abundance. But from those who are unfaithful, even what little they have will be taken away. Now throw this useless servant into outer darkness, where there will be weeping and gnashing of teeth.'" *Matthew 25:14-30*

This parable describes the consequences of two attitudes toward Christ's return. The person who diligently prepares for it by investing his or her time and talents to serve God will be rewarded. The person who has no heart for the work of the Kingdom will be punished. God rewards faithfulness. Those who bear no fruit for God's Kingdom cannot expect to be treated the same as those who are faithful.

"A rich man hired a manager to handle his affairs, but soon a rumor went around that the manager was thoroughly dishonest. So his employer called him in and said, 'What's this I hear about your stealing from me? Get your report in order, because you are going to be dismissed.'

"The manager thought to himself, 'Now what? I'm through here, and I don't have the strength to go out and dig ditches, and I'm too proud to beg. I know just the thing! And then I'll have plenty of friends to take care of me when I leave!'

"So he invited each person who owed money to his employer to come and discuss the situation. He asked the first one, 'How

much do you owe him?' The man replied,
'I owe him eight hundred gallons of olive
oil.' So the manager told him, 'Tear up that
bill and write another one for four hundred
gallons.'

" 'And how much do you owe my employer?'
he asked the next man. 'A thousand bushels
of wheat,' was the reply. 'Here,' the manager
said, 'take your bill and replace it with one
for only eight hundred bushels.'

"The rich man had to admire the dishonest rascal for being so shrewd. And it
is true that the citizens of this world are
more shrewd than the godly are. I tell
you, use your worldly resources to benefit
others and make friends. In this way, your
generosity stores up a reward for you in
heaven.

"Unless you are faithful in small matters,
you won't be faithful in large ones. If you
cheat even a little, you won't be honest
with greater responsibilities. And if you are
untrustworthy about worldly wealth, who
will trust you with the true riches of

heaven? And if you are not faithful with other people's money, why should you be trusted with money of your own?

"No one can serve two masters. For you will hate one and love the other, or be devoted to one and despise the other. You cannot serve both God and money."
Luke 16:1-13

> We are to make wise use of the financial opportunities we have, not to earn heaven but to help people find Christ. If we use our money to help those in need or to help others find Christ, our earthly investment will bring eternal benefit. When we obey God's will, the unselfish use of possessions will follow.

If you have enjoyed reading the Bible passages presented in *Living Words of Jesus,* you can experience the entire text of the New Living Translation through any one of these quality editions:

DELUXE TEXT EDITION

The *Holy Bible,* Deluxe Text Edition, is perfect for anyone who wishes to experience God's Word through the New Living Translation. It features clear, easy-to-read type and a beautiful, long-lasting binding.

LIFE APPLICATION STUDY BIBLE

This best-selling study Bible contains over 10,000 Life Application™ notes to help you apply the truth of God's Word to everyday life.

TOUCHPOINT BIBLE

The *TouchPoint Bible* quickly directs you to specific passages in God's Word on hundreds of topics you are most likely to face.

NEW BELIEVER'S BIBLE

The *New Believer's Bible* presents
the basics of Christianity in a
way that is easy to follow and
understand. Also available in a
New Testament edition.

THE ONE YEAR BIBLE

Through a simple and easy-to-use
format, *The One Year Bible* gives you
an organized method of reading
through the entire Bible in one year!

BIBLE ON CASSETTE

The beauty and style
of the New Living
Translation comes alive
through this dramatic,
multivoice presentation.